GWEN SMITH

Broken into Beautiful

HARVEST HOUSE PUBLISHERS
EUGENE, OREGON

This book contains some stories in which the author has changed people's names and some details of their situations in order to protect their privacy.

Published in association with William K. Jensen Literary Agency, 119 Bampton Court, Eugene, Oregon 97404.

Cover by Left Coast Design, Portland, Oregon

BROKEN INTO BEAUTIFUL
Copyright © 2008 by Gwen Smith
Published by Harvest House Publishers
Eugene, Oregon 97402
www.harvesthousepublishers.com

Library of Congress Cataloging-in-Publication Data
Smith, Gwen, 1970-
Broken into beautiful / Gwen Smith.
    p. cm.
ISBN 978-0-7369-2317-0 (pbk.)
ISBN 978-0-7369-3421-3 (eBook)
1. Christian women—Religious life. 2. Spiritual healing. I. Title.
BV4527.S627 2008
248.8'43—dc22
                                                                2008012053

Printed in the United States of America

17 18 / VP-SK / 13 12

Contents

1. Behind the Smile 7

2. Worthless into Precious 23

3. Guilty to Forgiven 37

4. Hungry into Satisfied 57

5. Empty into Full 77

6. Shattered Matters 93

7. Secrets and Accusations 111

8. Measuring Up 125

9. Valued and Adored 139

10. Got Beauty? 157

    Notes 174

With Heartfelt Thanks

First, to my husband, Brad: You are my best friend, lifetime love, and all-around favorite person on the planet. Thanks for encouraging me to chase God's heart with my life and for modeling what that looks like each day.

To my fabulously fun children: You challenge me to laugh, love, and live with great adventure! Thanks for giving me hugs, kisses, and grace whenever I need it. I love you guys more than I could possibly express.

Preston, my competitive, all-sports boy, I'll always love you the longest. You make daddy and me so proud. You are a gentle, honest, and responsible leader.

Hunter, my cuddly bubba, thanks for making meal times fun with your wacky faces and silly grin, for being tenderhearted, and for showing the world that white boys really *can* have rhythm. You are a brave, bright, and bubbly boy.

Kennedy, my sweet mini-me, thank you for helping me see the world through your fresh, vibrant, artistic eyes. I love your creativity and sense of style. You are my precious, loved, and beautiful princess.

To Bill Jensen: You believed in this book before it was written and in me before you knew I could write. Thanks for always being available, for your guidance, for your fish stories, and for your pep talks. You are more than just my agent; you are my friend.

To my girlfriends: What would I do without you? Tara, Susan, Kathy, Maria, Micca, Kristina, Elise, Amy, Lauren, Haven, Cindi, Kristal, Peg, Carol, Michelle, Erin, Ellen, Lisa, Chris, Jacki, Suzanne, Melinda, Rachel, Marian, Daphne, Sally, Lysa, Renee, Genia, Heather, Jen, Sarah, Kerry, Jenny, Tammy, Betsy, and to my Girlfriends in God, Sharon and Mary—I love you, I love you, I love you! I'm so glad we do life together.

To MaryLou and Jerry Eisaman: I love you, Mom and Dad! To have praying, God-fearing parents is a special gift. You are true blessings in my life. Thank you for loving me, no matter what.

To Grandma Adams: You are sunshine in my heart. Thank you for being a godly example to me and to our entire family.

To Rod Morris: Thanks for making what I write better. You are a man of great detail and skill. It has been a delight to work with you from the very start.

To the entire Harvest House staff: Thank you for believing in the message of this book and for the work you do on a daily basis to make the fame of Jesus known.

Special thanks to: Allyson Werner, Tara Dye, Melody Hogan, Suzanne Boyd, Denise Hammond, Melissa George, Rosetta Woods, Lysa TerKeurst, Renee Swope, Brad and Jamie Bailey, Debbie Bagwell, and Danita Hiles. Thank you for allowing your stories to be used for God's glory.

To Sue Smith and Chad Cates: Thank you for linking arms with me to bring lyric and melody to *Broken into Beautiful.* God is on the move with this message...and it all started with our song.

To Dave Clark and the Sunday Best Music team: I love working with you guys! Thanks for dreaming with me, for trusting my instincts, and for supporting me every step of the way. You are like family, and I love you all.

To my Life Fellowship family: Pastor Bobby, Pastor Roland, Brad, and Ryan—thanks for your prayers, for allowing me to take over the back room, and for all the free cups of coffee. Worship team and Life group—y'all rock! Thanks for all of your prayers and support.

Finally, to my grace-filled Savior, Jesus Christ: You have changed my worthless into precious, my guilty to forgiven, my hungry into satisfied, and my empty into full. Thank You for restoring the broken places of my life and transforming them into a display of Your beauty and splendor.

1

Behind the Smile

Those who look to him are radiant;
their faces are never covered with shame.

PSALM 34:5

I should begin with a confession: I've spent most of my life hiding behind a smile. You know that saying, "My life is an open book"? Well, it never really applied to me. My life has been more of a partially opened book. While I've shared satisfying successes, tear-filled trials, and entertaining experiences over the years, I've kept most of the shadier happenings of my life under wraps in a prideful attempt to save face.

Nice admission for a woman in ministry, huh?

I've always considered my past just that: my past. I'm pragmatic that way. I've experienced shame, pain, and brokenness as much as the next person. I just haven't been in the habit of sharing the particulars with people who could possibly judge me for it. God has graciously rescued me from the pits that I've fallen in—and I'm thankful that He has—but I've never wanted to chat with people about the darker details. I'm a smiler by nature. I have a positive, upbeat personality. It's *my* stuff. People don't need to know my stuff, right? Right.

So why the book?

The simple answer is this: God has called me to a higher level of transparency in ministry. While you may never have to share your stuff with masses of women, I must if I am to obey Him. God has written His restoring, unconditional love into every broken paragraph of every broken chapter of who I am. I've spent my entire adult life fearfully flipping past pages that tell of the failures and struggles I've been through.

Not anymore.

It's time for my life to become an open book.

Time to get real.

An Average American Girl

I grew up in Mayberry. Well, the town was actually called Irwin, but comparatively it was Mayberry.

In the summers, my brothers, sisters, and I spent our days outside in the blazing sun, playing barefoot in freshly cut grass. We enjoyed big Fourth of July parades, drank large amounts of ice-cold lemonade, attended huge family reunions, and ate our weight in fresh tomatoes and homegrown sweet corn.

In the fall, we rooted for both the Steelers and our high school football team, went trick or treating, raked endless piles of colorful leaves (then jumped in them, of course), and sipped warm apple cider as often as we could get our mom to buy it.

Each blustery Pennsylvania winter, we had pictures taken on Santa's lap, shoveled ridiculous amounts of snow, and rooted for our high school basketball team. We drank mug-after-mug of hot chocolate with mini-marshmallows, waited on pins and needles to see if Punxsutawney Phil saw his shadow on Groundhog Day, and ate many bowls of tummy-warming chili with buttered saltines on the side.

Our springs were filled with Easter programs at church, bulb planting at home, and great anticipation of the last day of school.

The people were kind, the houses were modest, and the community was committed to clean living. That meant different things to different people, but for my family it meant going to church, washing behind our ears, and applying the Golden Rule. Basically, I come from your average middle-class American family and your average hard-working American town.

I am the middle child of five, born to my parents in eight short years. We squabbled like normal siblings, shared bedrooms, and often fought for our parents' attention, but overall we enjoyed the benefits of being raised in a large family. We had quirky family jokes (someone would ask, "Who lives in that house?" and another would reply "Howard Ino?") and favorite family movies (*The Sound of Music* and, forgive me for this one, *The Jerk*). We had a kind, practical, and godly mom who kept the house running smoothly as best she could and a strong yet silly dad who worked hard and loved to tease us. We always had a roof over our heads, a hot meal on the table, and clothes on our backs (even if they were hand-me-downs). We were very blessed.

From the time I was little, I loved going to church. I didn't necessarily love wearing a dress like my mom always wanted me to, but I loved church. I loved the singing, the flannelgraph Sunday school lessons, the Bible games, and my friends. I loved Mr. Dunn, my Sunday school teacher. He was always quick with a smile that was warm like a blanket. Each Sunday he would share a simple gospel message and then ask us if we wanted to accept Christ as our Savior. With our small heads bowed, he would lead us in the sinner's prayer. I'm certain there will be a long line of people in heaven thanking Mr. Dunn for his faithful service and life-changing prayers. I'll be one of them.

So before braces ever graced my teeth, I had a smile that shone for the Lord. It was a buck-toothed smile, but a smile nonetheless. I became a Christian in Mr. Dunn's Sunday school class when I was just nine years old. To me, faith was pretty simple. I knew that I regularly made mistakes and bad choices, which the Bible calls sin, and even though I was young, I knew that I could not measure up to the perfect standard of a holy God. So when I learned of this God-man named Jesus—who came from heaven to earth, lived a perfect, sinless life, suffered and died in my place, rose from the dead, and then ascended into heaven, *all so I could be forgiven*—it was pretty much a no-brainer to my nine-year-old self. I confessed my sin, asked to be forgiven, and embraced the joy that had been placed in my heart.

I was His and He was mine…simple as that. I have loved God since I was a child.

The Drama Angel

I've also loved music and sports. I sang my first solo when I was ten. It was for the 1980 West Hempfield Elementary School fifth and sixth grade Christmas pageant. The program was called "The Blue Angel." I was the blue angel. Now, you might think that I would have been excited to be the blue angel, but I was actually miffed about it because I had previously auditioned for a speaking part and was told that I would be a princess in Act III of the play. A princess! My heart soared when I found out that I had won a speaking role. I had always wanted to be a beautiful princess. What little girl doesn't? I threw down a serious happy dance that day. Life was good. I went home and spent that entire evening in my bedroom, going over my lines and prepping for my theatrical debut.

The very next day at school came a fateful call to the principal's office. I remember it as if it were yesterday. My pulse raced as I walked down the hall toward the curious meeting. Once I got there, I was asked to sit in one of the plastic chairs outside Mr. Welty's office. I waited for what seemed like forever, and when I was finally called in, I saw Mr. Welty, Mrs. Downs (the music teacher), and Mrs. MacDonald (the PTA president). They said the usual pleasantries and then dove right into a conversation that wrecked my plans and broke my little heart. They wanted me to be the blue angel instead of a princess.

"What?" I said. "Why? I really *want* to be a princess! I auditioned for the part and was chosen. Why do you want me to be the blue angel?"

Mr. Welty patiently explained that Mrs. Downs had just informed both him and Mrs. MacDonald that I had a pretty singing voice, and they really needed a good singer for the song of the blue angel. They said there was only one song in the play and *I* would get to sing it. But all I heard was that I would not get to be a princess. I reluctantly agreed to be the blue angel, left the office with my head hung low, and cried the whole way back to my classroom.

My flare for drama was in full swing when they phoned my mother a few days later and told her that, as the blue angel, I had to wear a light blue, flowing dress. A sissy dress! As a card-carrying member of the tomboy club, I was fit to be tied. I hated dresses and was mad as a hornet. I thought the whole play would be a big mess and that they had made a huge mistake by making me sing.

Eventually, the big night came. I swallowed my pride about the dress and got through the song. The program was the talk of the elementary school, and I had now been formally initiated into public singing. From that night on, whenever a solo needed to be sung, I was a prime candidate. Dress or no dress.

Steps of Faith

Life went on, and before I knew it I was in the awkward junior high years struggling with normal teenage girl issues: buck teeth, braces, boys, backstabbing, bras, and boobs. (Can I say *boobs* in a Christian book? *Anyhoo,* moving on...) I got along with most everyone except my siblings. On good days we hung out, played, and had lots of fun; on bad days we fought like cats and dogs. Normal, right? I was not perfect by any stretch, just your basic good kid who made relatively good decisions.

I was blessed to have been active in my church youth group from the time I was twelve through college. It was in youth group that I became deeply rooted in my walk with Christ and began to understand that my faith should show in my actions and decisions. There's a funky-cool Christian song by Nicole C. Mullen that poignantly says: "You can't get to heaven on granny's angel." I love that. My profession of faith was sincere as a nine-year-old, but as a teen I embraced faith in Christ as *mine*...not as my family heritage but as a very personal faith.

I was (and, to some degree, still am) quite the sassy girl. And though I was a believer, I had the normal teenage/parent "mouthy" issues and countless other rough edges that needed smoothing. I went through small bouts of rebellion and was romanced by a few things the world had to offer. But all in all, I was romanced by the Lord so much more.

One of the highlights of summer was always youth camp. We washed cars, sold hoagies, and babysat like crazy to raise money toward camp tuition. Each year, on a smoldering hot July day, we traveled across the long and winding Pennsylvania turnpike in a rickety old church bus that eventually delivered us to a church camp in the wooded hills of Carlisle. The trips up were always electric. Excitement sat in every seat. Even the peskiest of youth group boys were somewhat tolerable on the way because we bore a grace that accompanies focused anticipation. There was fun to be had, games to be played, and boys to be kissed at church camp. But more than that, when I was at camp I experienced God and worshiped with a passion that seemed incomparable to anything back home.

It was at church camp during the summer of 1984 that God placed a call on my life to serve Him in ministry. He spoke to my heart. No audible voice was necessary. *I knew that I knew that I knew* in my heart that God was calling me to join Him in a special way. I didn't know specifics, but I did know that I was to sing for Him, and Him only, for the rest of my life.

I began to write songs and jot down observations of life that moved me. My songs and writings were private, like a journal, so I kept them tucked away in a folder. A safe little folder. They were thoughts and songs just for me, or so I thought at the time. In reality, God had given me a talent to write. A talent that He would later require me to share with the world for Him.

I was an athletic youngster. Sports came naturally to me. My father was a great athlete too, and he still held a few track records at our high school when I attended twenty-five years later. I played anything and everything—softball, basketball, volleyball, and track. If a backyard football game was being played, I'd jump in on that too.

I eventually earned a full scholarship to play volleyball at a Division I university in Ohio. Of all the sports I played, volleyball was my passion. I loved the game and the high level of competition.

So off to college I went as a mostly innocent, God-loving, hardworking teenager who had said yes to the cross and no to the crowd.

I was a girl with convictions. A girl of strong disciplines. A girl of high moral standards. A girl who walked the straight and narrow. I was a virgin.

Good start, huh?

Don't be too impressed. College was the place where my faith collided with the temptations that led me to choices that altered the course of my life and landed me in a pit of despair.

Season of Compromise

So how does a girl who loves God and comes from a loving, stable home find herself wading through muck and mire in the pit of broken-ness? How is it possible that a girl who longed to do right and honor Christ with her life could end up in an abortion clinic at the age of twenty? And how is it conceivable that a young lady who made such horrible and murderous decisions could be reconciled to a holy God in heaven?

I never meant to stray from my values. I went off to college and began a new chapter in life, one that I thought I could handle on my own. I continued to say yes to God about some things, like going to church every Sunday and being involved in campus ministry. But I also began to say yes to the world about other things, like having a drink at a party or messing around with my boyfriend. I was still the same Gwen, just a compromised version of me. It was a gradual thing. I was the frog in a pot of cool water over a low flame that eventually became frog soup.

My career as a college athlete brought many blessings and many challenges. One major blessing was a full scholarship that saved my parents and me thousands of dollars each year. It gave me a promising post-college future without debt from student loans. Blessings were also found in the close friendships I formed with a few of my team-mates and in the game itself. I flat-out love to play volleyball.

There were a few significant challenges as well. I played under a coach who had little respect or tolerance for people of faith. He was from a communist European country and had a potpourri of theological convictions that he had gathered along the way—mainly *secular humanism* with a touch of *new age* thrown in for good measure. Consequently, he and I were not tight chums. I became the token Christian, the virgin, the good girl on the team.

All of that pressure made my season of compromise even tougher. I felt obligated to hide behind a plastic smile so as not to mess up my Sandra Dee persona. So my sophomore year, when I handed my purity over to my boyfriend, I kept it a secret. It was nobody's business but mine. Eventually, secrets and compromise became comfortable to me. I wore them like a pair of faded jeans. If I drank at a party, cheated on a test, or slept with my boyfriend, I was discreet.

My boyfriend and I were in love. Though we knew it was not God's plan for us to have sex outside of marriage, and though we tried to control our passion, we often found ourselves surrendering to the moment. We were Christians. It drove us nuts! We didn't want to grieve the heart of God. We went to church together and prayed that God would give us strength to make pure decisions, but we kept falling into the familiar trap of our sin.

In the middle of my junior year, the compromises and choices that my boyfriend and I had made resulted in a pregnancy. When the stick turned blue that cold winter morning, my heart turned black. I thought my life was over. I had disgraced my family and my faith. I felt like the world's largest phony and could hardly stand to be me. It was unbearable.

My mind flooded with consequences that I had no desire to consider.

What choice do I have? I thought. *If I actually have this baby, I'll lose my volleyball scholarship. I'd have to drop out of college. I'd be the topic of campus gossip. I'd publicly disgrace my family and my faith. People would know that I had been having sex! My secrets would no longer be secrets.*

I couldn't let that happen. I just couldn't.

I reacted by rushing past the values I had been raised with, the convictions of my heart, and the fundamentals of my faith to the blurred "solution" of death. I had never accepted that abortion was a moral option for an unplanned pregnancy until it was *my* unplanned pregnancy.

I remember the phone call to my boyfriend. Through sobs, I managed to tell him I was pregnant. There was a long pause on the other end of the phone…and then came the speed round of questions and comments: "What are we going to do? Do you think we should get married? Oh, my gosh…oh, my gosh…what are we going to do? Do you want to have this baby? What are we going to do? What about volleyball? What will your parents say? What will my parents say? Oh, my gosh!"

Like trapped animals, we were frantically looking for a way out. Then we made our decision. We would take care of it. It wasn't time for us to have a baby yet.

God wasn't consulted. He wasn't invited into our decision.

Adam and Eve hid in the garden after eating the forbidden fruit. My boyfriend and I hid from God and did what we considered to be our only option. We made a plan. He would pick me up and take me to a clinic that I read about in the yellow pages.

When the day came, we drove in icy silence. I was Fort Knox. No one was going to break through the protective walls I had constructed.

You see, there was never a moment that I believed having an abortion was the right thing to do. I only stubbornly and naively believed that my choice was the only ladder out of the horrible pit I had dug for myself.

I was wrong. Dead wrong.

There, in the sterile room of that stale clinic, I used an alias. I wasn't Gwen. My charts did not say that I was Gwen, the girl who was raised by good parents, the girl who was raised in the Word of God to know right from wrong. The counselor I had met with said that using my name could have made me feel uncomfortable with the "harmless and legal procedure" I was having done that day. Nobody else needed to know. I was anonymous.

It was my secret. A secret of chains that bound me in silence for the ensuing fifteen years. A secret kept because I mistakenly assumed that no one else could handle the ugly truth of my sinfulness with grace and forgiveness. I was a Christian girl. Christians don't get pregnant when they aren't married, and Christians don't have abortions, right? It was all too scandalous, and I was crazy afraid of the consequences.

Most of that day was a blur. It was a dark, cold January day. Though the clinic was lit with bright fluorescent lights, the flame of dignity and hope in my heart had grown dim. I blocked out all the voices in my head as they contested what I was doing. I was desperate and scared.

I was Peter. Simon Peter was a fisherman Jesus had called to be a fisher of men. His relationship with Christ was passionate and intimate, but far from perfect. He was a disciple, one of Jesus' closest friends. Jesus called Peter "the rock," and he would eventually go on to build the foundation of the Christian church.

But before he did, the Bible shows us, in Luke 22:54-60, that the night Jesus was arrested, Peter "followed at a distance," sat in a courtyard with enemies of Jesus, and denied three times the Lord he loved. Remarkably, Jesus *knew* Peter would betray Him, yet still extended advanced mercy as He said to him, "Simon, Simon, Satan has asked to sift you as wheat. But I have prayed for you, Simon, that your faith may not fail. And when you have turned back, strengthen your brothers" (Luke 22:32).

I imagine that when Peter betrayed Jesus on that long, dark night preceding the crucifixion, he must have felt a physical illness and emotional angst similar to the one that shattered my life the day I said yes to death and betrayed my Lord. Luke 22:62 tells us that after he had disowned Jesus three times, Peter "went outside and wept bitterly."

Peter *knew* Jesus, yet still betrayed Him.

He *loved* Jesus.

I *knew* Jesus, yet still betrayed Him.

I *loved* Jesus too.

A Broken Heart

But that love was tucked into the icy trunk of my heart on that snowy winter afternoon.

For weeks following my abortion, I went through each day under a dark cloud of despair. I couldn't reconcile what I had done with who I was and who I was supposed to be. My heart was broken. I felt hopeless and was horribly ashamed. I was disgusted and lost. I remember fighting with my roommates about things that really didn't matter and fighting with my boyfriend about most anything. My poor roommates had no idea why I'd turned into Cruella DeVille. I was irrational and angry 24/7. I hated what I had done, and I hated myself for doing it. I was responsible for the death of my baby. It was my fault and I knew it.

And it haunted me.

Voices of accusation screamed in my head. *Murderer! Baby killer! Hypocrite! You can never tell a soul about this!* Condemnation from the accuser kept me shackled. Without realizing it, I was a captive to my own acceptance of his words.

The dark days turned into weeks, which turned into months. Although I could turn on the fake charm like water from a faucet— oh, how my plastic smile served me well in those days!—I was dying inside. At night, my pillow soaked up rivers of tears. I would lie awake, wondering if my baby was a boy or girl, or if my baby had felt any pain as she was being sucked from my body.

I wept. I wept for both my baby and for myself. It was necessary. It felt right to cry. And though the tears helped my soul grieve, none were as healing as the ones I cried to Jesus when I finally turned back to Him.

A New Song

Like Peter after the rooster crowed, I wept bitterly at the feet of Jesus in raw repentance. Then, as the psalmist did,

> I waited patiently for the LORD;
> > he turned to me and heard my cry.
> He lifted me out of the slimy pit,
> > out of the mud and mire;
> he set my feet on a rock
> > and gave me a firm place to stand.
> He put a new song in my mouth,
> > a hymn of praise to our God.
> Many will see and fear
> > and put their trust in the LORD.
>
> > (PSALM 40:1-3)

And though I didn't deserve His mercy, Jesus forgave me. My forgiveness was immediate and complete, but the healing took time. He eventually did give me a new song.

> Who is a God like you,
> > who pardons sin and forgives the transgression
> > of the remnant of his inheritance?
> You do not stay angry forever
> > but delight to show mercy.
>
> > (MICAH 7:18)

Who is this God who forgives *all* of our wretchedness?

How could He?

Although I knew I was forgiven, I wrestled with these perplexing questions for years. I accepted most of His truth, but a disquieting voice hung around to tell me time and time again, "You are now disqualified for anything of significant kingdom value because of what you have done. You had your chance and you blew it."

It wasn't the voice of God.

I recognize now that it was the voice of the accuser.

Have you heard that voice? If so, tell him to stop talking! Listen to God's voice, the voice of Truth. The Bible assures us that our hope has *never been about what we have done; it has always been about what*

Christ has done. "For it is by grace you have been saved, through faith—and this not from yourselves, it is the gift of God—not by works, so that no one can boast" (Ephesians 2:8-9).

Friend, accept God's gift of grace today. He wants so badly to give it to you. It's free, but it was bought at a very high price.

It is extravagant. Unwrap it. Embrace it. Live with it.

Embracing God's Restoration

When I was twenty-nine years old (nine years after my abortion) God called me to His service again. He gently reminded my heart that when He calls you, you are called. The great commission is for all of us, not for the perfect among us. Mistakes don't change that commission. There may be a time of healing, restoration, and discipline, but God can and will still use you.

Did you hear that?

God can use each and every person who surrenders her brokenness into His hands...no matter what. That is what the good news of Jesus is all about! The Bible is filled with people just like you and me who failed miserably, wounded themselves and others, and were still met with divine mercy. David was known as "a man after God's own heart," but he had a scandalous affair with a married woman and then murdered her innocent husband. Mercy met him at his deepest need. Mercy longs to meet each of us at our deepest need and bids us to come.

Have you met with mercy? Have you experienced God's compassion and forgiveness?

Once I understood that I was still called, I desperately sought God's will for my life. I knew my heritage in faith, but I wanted to leave a clear legacy. His Word reminded me in Romans 8:1-2 that "there is now no condemnation for those who are in Christ Jesus, because through Christ Jesus the law of the Spirit of life set me free from the law of sin and death." Forgiveness freed me to respond to God's call and to step out in faith.

So I did. I said yes to God. I told Him I would do what He wanted me to do. And after I said yes to God, my journey became rich in love. I began to experience God on a whole new level. I still made mistakes, and I still failed regularly as a wife, mother, and friend. But the more I grew in Christ, the less I seemed to fail. Not because of anything good in me, but because of Christ in me.

Blessings followed the surrender. I embraced my forgiveness and got busy for God. I wrote songs, led worship, recorded CDs, and told people about the unconditional love of God. I did all that He was calling me to, and I was willing to do most anything He asked of me. But I was *not* telling anyone about my abortion. That was not an option.

I had been healed and restored from deep spiritual and emotional wounds, yet for fifteen years I wasn't willing to tell anybody. I had held tightly to my secret for so long that my stubborn grasp did not release easily. As I grew in Christ, the Holy Spirit began to nudge me to talk about my abortion. I wrestled with God about this. We went countless rounds. I'm embarrassed to say that thousands of tears fell, and my pride had to be continually crushed before I conceded.

A Willing Heart

God asked that I be willing to tell so that others could know forgiveness and healing as I do. It made sense, but oh, it was hard!

God *should* have my willingness. It's nothing compared to His sacrifice.

Now I am willing. It took me a long time to get here, but I'm willing. A great responsibility comes with this forgiveness. I do not think that we are obligated to recklessly share all of our stuff with others just because we are believers. I am convinced, however, that if God is calling us to use something for His purposes, then—as His children, saved by grace—we *are* obligated to obey Him.

I'm not sure what this might mean in your life, but I suspect the Holy Spirit might just be stirring something deep within your heart right now. My friend, is there something that God is calling you to do for Him? How has the unconditional love of God affected who you are? Are you willing to step past your fears to walk in obedience? It is time, as Jesus said to Peter, "to turn to [our] companions and give them a fresh start" (Luke 22:32, MSG) through the testimonies of our lives. It's time to embrace the brokenness of our past and view it as an opportunity to do good.

The guilt, pain, and shame of our pasts tell us we are disqualified to move on, to serve God, to be free, and to know peace. But to believe this lie is to believe that your sin is outside the scope of God's grace. Nothing could be further from the truth. You have purpose in this life. And though you may have gone through a season of hurt, rejection, or pain, God can and will pick you up and place you back on track.

There is no condemnation for those in Christ. While the enemy loves to cast false guilt, our Lord loves to extend grace and forgiveness, which is the remedy that restores all our broken pieces. Don't hold onto those pieces. Don't hide them behind a plastic smile. Bring them into the light, lay them at the feet of Jesus, and let go.

Then stand back and watch the wonder of grace at work as God creates something beautiful in you.

"Broken into Beautiful"

Gwen Smith, Sue Smith, Chad Cates

She's smiling on the outside,
But she's hurting on the inside.
It's getting hard just living anymore.
And the shadows she has clung to,
Painful things that she has been through,
Have left her feeling worthless, Lord…but

You change worthless into precious,
Guilty to forgiven,
Hungry into satisfied,
Empty into full.
All the lies are shattered,
And we believe we matter
When You change broken into beautiful.

We live with accusations,
Sometimes heavy expectations,
That tell us we can never measure up.
And yet You repeat with mercy
That in Your eyes we are worthy
At last we see how much we're loved 'cause
Though we can't see how we can stand before You, Lord
And feel valued, priceless and adored

[Chorus]

2
Worthless into Precious

*"You are precious and
honored in my sight…"*

ISAIAH 43:4A

I recently bought my daughter a really cute jacket at the mall. It's a hoodie that's made of a cuddly fabric with cream, lavender, and mint-green horizontal stripes. The jacket zips up in the front and is well crafted, stylish, and simply adorable.

When I bought it, I thought the price was fair, so I gladly pulled out my wallet and paid the amount. I was a kid in a candy store on the way home. I fully anticipated a shriek of happiness from my little bag of beans when I gave it to her. I wasn't disappointed. Kennedy loved her new coat, and I was pleased with my purchase. Happy dances all around…until a week later when I saw the same jacket in the same store at a greatly reduced price. Are you tensing up with me? Suddenly, I felt snookered. Ripped off. Taken advantage of. As soon as I saw the red line on the price tags of the unsold coats, everything changed. Kennedy's jacket wasn't worth what I paid for it.

When we speak of the *worth* of something, we often consider it a relative term, one that has shifting factors. Last week the cute jacket was $39, and now it's $19.99. The jacket didn't change, but its perceived worth did.

Now, consider the worth of a woman. Is her value based upon variable, shifting factors or is it based upon fixed factors? Seems to be a silly question, doesn't it? Fixed, of course! But if the answer is so glaringly obvious, why do we as women struggle so much with feeling worthless? Why do we walk around feeling like I felt toward that marked-down jacket? I think it's because we often allow variable earthly factors to define our worth.

What kind of variable factors? Women feel worthless for many reasons:

- They've been *abused* (raped, molested, physically abused, verbally abused)

- They've *been told* they're worthless (by a parent, spouse, sibling, teenage child)

- They've made *poor choices* (divorce, infidelity, abortion, promiscuity, eating disorders, addictions, uncontrolled anger)

- They've been *cheated on* (infidelity, Internet affair, pornography)

- They're *codependent* (determine their value based upon other people: "If my husband isn't okay, I'm not okay.")

- They *don't collect a paycheck* (stay-at-home moms that have left the work force, laid-off employees, displaced employees, those on disability)

- They've battled an *illness* (unable to care for family, perform basic home duties, participate in ministry or Bible study like they used to, can't drive or cook)

Unfortunately, the factors that we use to define our worth are almost endless. Many of us have felt ignored, invisible, insignificant, useless, undesired, ugly, unloved, or forgotten. We girls are emotional, broken in many ways. Great portions of our identity and of our personal value are wrapped into combustible packages of emotion…how we *feel* about this or that. The truth is, our worth has nothing to do with our feelings.

Trust me, I'm not going to try to convince you that I know everything there is to know about feeling like a woman of worth. Or about *being* a woman of worth. I am in the trenches with you. I struggle with normal woman things. I don't live a fancy-schmancy, rose-colored wonder-life. I hit the snooze button several times each morning. I pack lunches for my kids. I waste countless hours each year sitting in the carpool line. It's a never-ending struggle for me to keep the laundry clean, and my kids often have to fish for a matching pair of socks in the clean-clothes basket. My husband is my soul mate, but he's far from perfect. For that matter, Brad should win a lifetime achievement award for enduring the drama of me! And my kids bring me both great joy *and* great frustration on a daily basis.

Is this sounding at all familiar to you?

See, I'm just like you, and I'm walking this faith journey right beside you. In fact, the more I know God, the less inclined I am to pretend to have life or faith figured out. Amen? I'm constantly tempted to define my worth with activities and accomplishments. I've come to realize, however, that way of thinking is a spiritual dead end. Scripture tells us that anything we do in our own strength or of our own goodness is of no value to God.

> All of us have become like one who is unclean, and *all our righteous acts are like filthy rags* (Isaiah 64:6a, emphasis mine).

What I do know is this: Because of Jesus Christ, and not because of anything else, I'm a woman of highest worth. I'm a grace girl. I'm not perfect by a long stretch, but I've been changed by the unconditional love of God and restored to perfect beauty through the shed blood of Jesus. Because of love, we are His daughters, precious in His sight. In light of this, we need to set aside feelings that diminish our value and embrace our proper identity: children of the King of Kings.

In his book, *The Search for Significance,* Robert McGee writes:

> For various reasons (family background, past experiences, poor modeling), we may have negative presumptions that determine our receptivity to love and truth. In some cases, God's light may not yet have penetrated to our deepest

thoughts and beliefs about ourselves. These past beliefs may not be clearly articulated but often reflect misperceptions such as these:

- God doesn't really care about me.
- I am an unlovable, worthless person.
- Nobody will ever love me.
- I'll never be able to change.
- I've been a failure all my life. I guess I'll always be a failure.

If people really knew me, they wouldn't like me.

When the light of love and honesty shines on thoughts of hopelessness, it is often very painful. We begin to admit that we really do feel negatively about ourselves—and have for a long time. But God's love, expressed through His people and woven into our lives by His Spirit and His Word, can, over a period of time, bring healing even to our deepest wounds and instill within us an appropriate sense of self-worth.[1]

I have witnessed this to be true time and time again, and it burns me up that the enemy has such a strong grip on God's daughters in this area. We need to associate the word *worthless* with the word *lie*. That's exactly what it is, a big fat lie! I talk to women all the time who bend a knee to negative feelings and live defeated lives because they don't know how to overcome their sense of worthlessness. What Robert McGee wrote is true: God wants every one of us to experience healing and have an appropriate sense of self-worth.

The Blurry Era

Have you ever felt alone, scared, angry, confused, and hurt all at the same time? Ever felt like running away from a difficult situation? I have. There was a time when I wanted to run—hard and fast—from life as I knew it. I was a young mom with three babies that had been born within three years and three months of each other. (A maternal trifecta!) Then, to everybody's surprise, my husband got a promotion that moved our seedling family across the country to a place where we didn't know anybody.

I jokingly refer to that time as the "blurry era." I had two babies in diapers that carried around their blankies, and one "big boy" who was potty training and struggling to say goodbye to his binky. There was always a diaper to change, a mouth to feed, or a mess to clean up. My days were a blur and my emotions were overloaded.

I was tired 24/7. Each day, Brad wore a suit, smelled of cologne, and drove to a sleek metropolitan high rise. I wore sweats, smelled of either throw up, baby food, or formula, and stayed home with three little humans who constantly cried, ate, played, made a mess, or slept (but never at the same time). Brad earned his company's President's Club Award that year. I earned our family's Pouter Club Award. I had left the work force and surrendered my weekly paycheck to wipe little bottoms and snotty noses. While I love my children dearly and did enjoy many sweet mommy moments, life didn't seem fair.

As a young mom, I regularly wrestled with my role in our family. My identity felt muted. Chained down. I felt that to embrace my position as a stay-at-home mom was the equivalent of hugging a porcupine. I didn't want to do it! I associated my worth with my work…and wrongly so. Sinfully so. I allowed my self-worth to be determined by variable factors. I felt less valuable as a woman, and I felt alone. In darker moments, I felt invisible and insignificant.

So many women struggle with these same feelings. Perhaps you are wrestling with feelings of insignificance right now. Allow these words of Jesus to turn your heart to the truth of your value:

> "Are not five sparrows sold for two pennies? Yet not one of them is forgotten by God. Indeed, the very hairs of your head are all numbered. Don't be afraid; you are worth more than many sparrows.

> "I tell you, whoever acknowledges me before men, the Son of Man will also acknowledge him before the angels of God" (Luke 12:6-8).

As I struggled to view myself as God did, He spoke truth to my heart through Scripture, and He used a friend to remind me of my value. He answered prayers that never even made it past my lips when he sent me a priceless girlfriend named Peg. She was a young mom, too, and we laughed together, cried together, prayed together, watched each other's children, and encouraged one another. She was a true blessing, my oasis in that desperate, dry desert season of my life.

Do you have friends like Peg? Are you that friend to anyone else? When we open our hearts and our homes to others, we can be used as vessels of encouragement and esteem.

> Two are better than one,
>> because they have a good return for their work:
> If one falls down,
>> his friend can help him up.
> But pity the man who falls
>> and has no one to help him up!
>
> (ECCLESIASTES 4:9-10)

God Loves and Pursues the Broken

Hagar was a young Egyptian servant girl who had some serious challenges. In the Old Testament book of Genesis, chapter 16, we hear of her plight...and of her flight:

> Now Sarai, Abram's wife, had borne him no children. But she had an Egyptian maidservant named Hagar; so she said to Abram, "The LORD has kept me from having children. Go, sleep with my maidservant; perhaps I can build a family through her."
>
> Abram agreed to what Sarai said. So after Abram had been living in Canaan ten years, Sarai his wife took her Egyptian maidservant Hagar and gave her to her husband to be his wife. He slept with Hagar, and she conceived (vv. 1-4a).

I imagine that Hagar grew up with low self-esteem. As a servant, she probably felt discarded, insignificant, and unimportant. Not only had she been sold to Abram and Sarai, but she was forced to become his wife as well. I don't know about you, but thinking about that makes my stomach do yucky flip-flops.

What do you think that conversation was like when Sarai commanded Hagar to sleep with her elderly husband? How do you think Hagar felt? I find it disturbing and unfair.

> When [Hagar] knew she was pregnant, she began to despise her mistress. Then Sarai said to Abram, "You are responsible for the wrong I am suffering. I put my servant in your arms, and now that she knows she is pregnant, she despises me. May the LORD judge between you and me."
>
> "Your servant is in your hands," Abram said. "Do with her whatever you think best." Then Sarai mistreated Hagar; so she fled from her (vv. 4b-6).

I can understand from a fleshly perspective why Hagar would choose to despise Sarai. When another person wrongs us, it's difficult to choose a godly, nonsassy response. We must be careful to pray for God's perspective and power so we don't allow weeds of resentment to overtake our hearts and guide our responses.

Hagar was a maidservant, a slave, who was forced to move to a foreign land and to sleep with the husband of her mistress. Though this was not an uncommon practice in that culture, there is still great uneasiness in my heart as I read what Hagar had to endure. She *was* mistreated—the Bible makes that clear—and she had fair reason to run. But God caught up with her not too far down the road.

> The angel of the LORD found Hagar near a spring in the desert; it was the spring that is beside the road to Shur. And he said, "Hagar, servant of Sarai, where have you come from, and where are you going?"
>
> "I'm running away from my mistress Sarai," she answered (vv. 7-8).

When faced with difficult circumstances, Hagar ran away. I might have done the same thing. But when she found herself seemingly alone in the desert, God sought her out and called her *by name.* The God of the universe knew Hagar's name. She was a slave, a nobody in the eyes of society, yet our God spoke lovingly through the angel of the Lord to this hurting mother-to-be and whispered promises of blessing to her weary heart.

> Then the angel of the LORD told her, "Go back to your mistress and submit to her." The angel added, "I will so increase your descendants that they will be too numerous to count" (vv. 9-10).

Stunned that the God of the universe cared to comfort her, Hagar responded by giving God a new name—El Roi, "the God Who Sees Me."

> She gave this name to the LORD who spoke to her: "You are the God who sees me," for she said, "I have now seen the One who sees me" (v. 13).

God pursued a broken woman and lifted her eyes to meet His own. He saw her in spite of who she was or thought herself to be, called her by name, and ministered to her heart. My heart burns with awe at the intimate intervention and tenderness that God showed Hagar, a grieving mom in a very dark hour.

Each one of us stumbles through the wilderness at times. Our unchanging God knows your name too. He sees you right where you are and knows the burdens of your heart. God sees each one of us just as He saw Hagar, and bids us to see ourselves through His eyes. Why would He? Because of Jesus. God sees you through the blood-stained curtain of Jesus Christ. Perfect. Forgiven. Precious.

> The LORD is close to the brokenhearted
> and saves those who are crushed in spirit.
>
> (PSALM 34:18)

There might be times when you feel alone and abandoned. In those times, it's important to remember that you are never beyond God's sight or out of His reach. There is no fleeing from His presence. In Psalm 139, David reminds us that God is everywhere:

> Where can I go from your Spirit?
>   Where can I flee from your presence?
> If I go up to the heavens, you are there;
>   if I make my bed in the depths, you are there.
> If I rise on the wings of the dawn,
>   if I settle on the far side of the sea,
> even there your hand will guide me,
>   your right hand will hold me fast.
>
> (PSALM 139:7-10)

God is inescapable. He loves you and He sees you. He is available to help you face trials with a courage that is firmly rooted in His strength and power so others might be drawn to Him and know His grace.

What can you learn from Hagar's encounter with God in the desert? Where have you come from and where are you going? So many times we want to run from our problems and sidestep accountability. Is there a difficulty in your life that you're tempted to run away from or ignore?

Debbie's Story

Debbie was a pastor's wife who felt worthless for years. She was verbally abused and emotionally abandoned in her marriage from the very beginning. She had been a virgin when she met her husband, so she knew something was very wrong when, seven months into their marriage, her husband went out of state for a "business trip" and gave Debbie a severe pelvic inflammatory disease when he got home.

Her doctors explained that she had gotten a bacterial infection that can only be sexually contracted. Debbie was hospitalized for five days and placed on strong medications. The IV antibiotics she received unknowingly rendered her birth control pills ineffective, and a pregnancy with their first child resulted. So Debbie stayed in the marriage, though she was wronged and mistreated.

"I was convinced that I deserved all that I encountered," Debbie said. "I also remember licking my wounds with thoughts like, *Well, at least I'm the wife, not the cheating lover.*"

The shame of it all kept Debbie silent and trapped in an unsafe marriage. Behind closed doors she endured verbal cruelty, and she believed the lies of her abuser. When her husband was in a good mood, things were good at home. But if he was in a foul mood, Debbie bore the brunt of his abuse and anger. Unfortunately, she endured the abuse for a long time before she left. Three kids, twenty-plus years, many affairs, and many lies later, Debbie finally had enough. She mustered up every ounce of courage she could find to leave and divorce her cheating, abusive, pastor husband.

You can imagine the scandal that took place in their church. Because the congregation was unaware of their pastor's abusive and immoral behavior, Debbie was victimized all over again in the court of public opinion. She bore the weight of public shame, humility, anger, accusations, rebellion from her children, and never-ending feelings of defeat and worthlessness. The weight of it all was heavy. So heavy that it pushed her into a deep pit of depression.

Debbie lost most everything in the divorce—her house, her identity, her financial stability, her dignity, and almost her sanity. In the aftermath, she even lost the intimate relationship she once had with Jesus Christ. She was still His daughter, saved by grace, but had run away from Him. Broken and angry, Debbie felt that God had let her down. She didn't understand how God—who is supposed to be good, who is supposed to hear our prayers, who is supposed to be our Protector and Defender—didn't protect her from the betrayal and the abuse. So, like Hagar, she ran to a desert to get away. Only Debbie ran to a desert of sin.

To soothe her pain, she temporarily turned to alcohol. The numbness she experienced from drinking brought an all-too-short reprieve from the sharp pains that pierced her heart when she was sober. And though she strayed from the heart of God and rebelled against His ways, He pursued her relentlessly. When she finally realized that her "victim mentality" had allowed her to trust a lying abuser instead of the God of truth, she turned back to the Lord.

In His mercy, God has restored Debbie's broken faith into a beautiful faith. He has redeemed her wounded heart and has filled her with His greater joy. And though, like all of us, she still experiences struggles and pain, by faith Debbie now embraces God's sovereignty and accepts His healing love. She is a changed woman. Changed by the unrelenting pursuit of God's unconditional love. Changed by the One who sees her as precious.

For a long time Debbie thought she was worthless because she was treated as if she were. She was told that she was. She believed what she heard from another person, even though what he said about her were lies. Debbie says, "I thought that I was a failure—that I didn't deserve to be loved with integrity, honesty, and faithfulness—that I caused my husband to sin and commit adultery because I wasn't good enough. I believed a whole pack of lies."

Other people can make us feel worthless. It happens all the time... even within the church. If you are in a relationship that beats you down and causes you to feel like dirt, in the name of Jesus reject the lies that are being projected on you. That's *not* who He says you are! If you are being mistreated or abused, tell a trusted friend, meet with your pastor, or get with a professional Christian counselor right away. And in all cases pray—without ceasing. Your abuser does not have the right to define who you are, to tell you what you think, to control or manipulate you, to tell you how you feel, or to condemn you for who you are or aren't. Only the God of heaven has the right to define you, and when you are in Christ, you are perfectly beautiful in His righteousness...not broken.

A Perfect Fit

So let's go back to Kennedy's new coat for just a moment. Imagine walking into God's department store. There on the rack you spy a coat that's just plain fabulous—I mean stop-you-in-your-tracks fabulous. *One-size fits all,* the tag reads. "Yeah, right," you whisper under your breath. Then you flip over the price tag and it's crazy expensive. Way beyond what you could ever dream of paying. Like if you added up every dollar that ever passed through your hands then multiplied that by ten thousand—that kind of expensive. Then imagine the store-owner walking over to you and slipping the coat off the rack and onto your shoulders.

"It's a perfect fit," he says with a smile.

"Sir," you manage to whisper, "I could never afford such a coat. This is meant for royalty and I'm, well, just an ordinary girl."

"Oh, precious woman, this coat is made especially for you, and the price has already been paid in full."

As the owner straightens the sleeves on your arms and adjusts the collar around your neck, you notice his hands…nail-pierced hands. And suddenly you realize that this is the covering you were meant to wear all along.

You see, the Bible tells us that because of what Jesus did on the cross, we can be clothed with the "robe of righteousness." The apostle Paul tells us that when we are reconciled to God, we become His righteousness. "God made him who had no sin to be sin for us, so that in him we might become the righteousness of God" (2 Corinthians 5:21).

There's no way we could ever afford or earn such a robe. But Jesus gave His life for us; He earned it for us. He paid the price and we receive the gift. Why? Because we are precious and highly valuable in the eyes of the One who Sees. And we never, never, never have to worry about being on anyone's bargain rack again.

> "Can a woman forget her nursing child
>> And have no compassion on the son of her womb?
>> Even these may forget, but I will not forget you.
> Behold, I have inscribed you on the palms of My hands."
>
> (ISAIAH 49:15-16, NASB)

"The One Who Sees Me"

Words by Gwen Smith, music by Brad Bailey

No matter where I am, Lord, You see me
No matter where I've been, You've been there too
And even in the times I feel abandoned and alone
You hold me like a child and draw me close to You

I lift my eyes to the One who sees me
No matter where I am
No matter where I am
I lift my soul to the One who lifts me
With a loving hand
With a loving hand
No matter where I am I'm turning to
The One who sees me

No matter what I say, Lord, You hear me
No matter where I go, You're by my side
And even in the times I feel exhausted and unheard
You love me with Your words, passionate and kind

[Chorus]

Even my darkest place is illuminated by Your grace
I'm so amazed

3

Guilty to Forgiven

Blessed is the man
whose sin the LORD does not count against him.

PSALM 32:2

Wouldn't it be cool if the world were perfect? Think about it. How fun would it be to have a perfect house, a perfect husband, perfect kids, and a perfect car? And how about a perfect figure, perfect friendships, perfect health, and a perfect heart?

Hmmmmm. That just sounds so foreign—so not real—yet so strangely familiar.

That's exactly the way our world began. Okay, I don't think Eve was overly concerned about her figure or her house, but her garden surely would've left Martha Stewart salivating. Not because Eve did anything to make the Garden of Eden fabulous, but because God made it perfect for her.

God created the world and everything in it, and it was good. Perfectly good. Then He put Adam in charge of all the earth, gave him a perfectly fabulous wife, and gave him one teeny, little instruction to follow.

> The LORD God took the man and put him in the Garden of Eden to work it and take care of it. And the LORD God commanded the man, "You are free to eat from any tree in the garden; but you must not eat from the tree of the knowledge of good and evil, for when you eat of it you will surely die" (Genesis 2:15-17).

Just one rule, that's all. Stay away from the fruit hanging from the tree of the knowledge of good and evil. How hard is that? Goodness gracious. You would think that something as big as the fall of man would've originated from more than a bite of a little piece of forbidden fruit. Doesn't it seem like a grander, more obnoxious rebellion should've been the landmark moment that changed our world? Yet how "fallen" of me to think that any one little disobedient act, one little sin, isn't all that big a deal. We'll learn from Adam and Eve that even a small amount of sin is deadly.

Everything was perfect until that fair afternoon when mother Eve took that very first bite of rebellion. That dreaded day when a piece of fruit caused the demise of the world. Wait a minute. The fall wasn't caused by a piece of fruit. It was caused by a heart that rebelled against God.

You know the story. It's Bible 101.

> Now the serpent was more crafty than any of the wild animals the LORD God had made. He said to the woman, "Did God really say, 'You must not eat from any tree in the garden'?"
>
> The woman said to the serpent, "We may eat fruit from the trees in the garden, but God did say, 'You must not eat fruit from the tree that is in the middle of the garden, and you must not touch it, or you will die.'"
>
> "You will not surely die," the serpent said to the woman. "For God knows that when you eat of it your eyes will be opened, and you will be like God, knowing good and evil."
>
> When the woman saw that the fruit of the tree was good for food and pleasing to the eye, and also desirable for gaining wisdom, she took some and ate it. She also gave some to her husband, who was with her, and he ate it. Then the eyes of both of them were opened, and they realized they were naked; so they sewed fig leaves together and made coverings for themselves.
>
> Then the man and his wife heard the sound of the LORD God as he was walking in the garden in the cool of the day, and

they hid from the LORD God among the trees of the garden (Genesis 3:1-8).

So after Adam and Eve ate the forbidden fruit, they hid from God. Okay, seriously, how ridiculous is that? As if God, the Creator of all things, couldn't see past a few trees. Good grief! It seems so silly, yet don't you and I do the same thing? When we sin, our gut response is to hide from God. To ignore our guilt. To crouch behind trees, as if God can't find us and doesn't know what we've done.

But, of course, God sees and knows everything.

God knew where Adam and Eve were the whole time. He also knew what they had done. Yet He pursued them with the purpose of restoring their relationship. He called out to His sinful children, "Where are you?" (v. 9).

Once they came out of hiding, they admitted their guilt to the Lord. After hearing their confessions and handing out consequences, "The LORD God made garments of skin for Adam and his wife and clothed them" (v. 21). He accepted their confessions of guilt, and then made a way for their shame to be covered.

Adam and Eve tried to cover up their shame by sewing fig leaves together. They tried to cover up their shame *on their own*. So many of us think that we can take care of our own messes and cover up our own sins. If we do enough good things in our lives, the bad will be outweighed. Through our own efforts, we sew fig leaves together and think we're covered. But our best efforts to cover our shame are still transparent and ineffective before God. Adam and Eve's fig coverings were severely lacking, so God covered them appropriately. Perfectly. In a way that only He could.

In order for garments of skin to be divinely fashioned, an innocent animal had to shed its blood. The death of that animal provided the means for Adam and Eve's clothes. Only three chapters into the history of mankind, we see the very first blood sacrifice. From that time on, God has always required a sacrifice of blood to atone for, to cover, our rebellious hearts.

The Bible calls our rebellion sin. Sin is described in a million different ways, but essentially it's missing the mark of perfection. In God's economy, if we miss the mark once, which we all do, we are in need of His covering. The good news is that God loves us so much, He made a way for our sins to be covered through the sacrifice of His perfect son, Jesus.

But let's not get ahead of ourselves here. If I start with the solution to our problem, I won't have a chapter to write! Let's talk more about this guilt thing. Adam and Eve's story of hiding from God reminds me of a story...

Caught Red-faced

When my three children were young, it was a challenge to keep track of where they were at all times. Brad and I baby-proofed the house as best we could and hoped for the best. I'll never forget the day that Preston and Kennedy were accounted for in the playroom, but Hunter had wandered off. I called for him but got no response.

I headed for the front staircase and listened for his little two-year-old voice. I checked his bedroom—no Hunter. I checked Preston's room—no Hunter. I checked Kennedy's room—no Hunter. By now, my heart was racing. As I headed into my bedroom, I began to hear faint noises from the master bathroom.

Our bathroom mirror gave me all the information I needed. Hunter had gotten into my red lipstick, and it was everywhere! I wanted to laugh; I wanted to cry. He was unaware of my presence as he continued his creative red-lipstick artwork on my walls and on the linen-closet door. On a whim, I ran quickly to get the camcorder.

Armed with stifled giggles and a video camera, I crossed the threshold of the bathroom and confronted my little chubby-cheeked, red-lipstick-all-over-his-face boy. He immediately hid his scandalous red tool behind his back. (At the age of two, he was already hiding behind that tree with Adam and Eve!) I asked him what he was doing, to which he replied, "Nothing." In my best trying-not-to-laugh mommy voice, I continued to ask him questions, and he continually denied any wrongdoing. (I really wish I could show you the video footage. It's hilarious! Sadly sinful, in a toddler kind of way, but hilarious.)

This makes me wonder how many times I have gone before the Lord in prayer holding my red lipstick behind my back. How many times have I—and do I—think I'm pulling one over on Him? Just as I saw the tangible evidence on Hunter's red face, God sees our hearts and knows what we've been up to. He sees pride, anger, gossip, and bitterness. He sees unforgiveness, unconfessed sins, the habits we cling to, the questionable shows we watch, the inappropriate flirtations, and the literature we read. He sees the failures that we try to hold behind our backs, and He lovingly invites us to come out of hiding so He can clean up the mess we've made.

Cleaning Up the Mess

The first step to cleaning up my toddler and my bathroom that day was to pitch the lipstick. Before the messes in our lives can be cleaned up, our red lipsticks need to be tossed as well. We need to come clean before God.

What is your red lipstick today?

Are you ready to hand it over to God?

Maybe you have handed it over to Him. Maybe you gave it to Him a long time ago. Even so, life remains messy until we die. Every day, the most faithful among us find new forbidden tubes of lipstick to dabble with. Whether our sins are blatantly obvious or discreet and teeny-tiny, we all need God to forgive us over and over again.

I'm so thankful that God is willing to forgive me over and over. That in spite of all I've done, He still loves me and is willing to hear my confessions of guilt. The Bible tells us that God forgives completely. "Therefore, since we have been justified through faith, we have peace with God through our Lord Jesus Christ, through whom we have gained access by faith into this grace in which we now stand" (Romans 5:1-2).

Do you know the completeness of His forgiveness? Do you know that peace?

Many Christians that I know are clothed in forgiveness by God with "perfect shame coverings," like the ones God provided to Adam and Eve, but they walk around as if they are still wearing their see-through, self-made, fig-leaf fashions. They hold God's peace at bay and hang on to their guilt.

A four-year-old girl was overheard reciting the Lord's Prayer, "and forgive us our trash baskets, as we forgive those who pass trash against us." When I first heard that story, I smiled. Then I thought of a conversation I had had recently with a girlfriend.

She's a Christian, but though she has "emptied her trash basket" of sin before the Lord in sincere repentance, she has not emptied the trash basket of self-condemnation. Not completely. She won't allow it. She struggles deeply to let go of mistakes she made in her past. She holds the trash basket lid on tightly. To be free of that waste doesn't seem fair in her mind.

She is haunted by shame. Haunted by sins that are no longer remembered by God. Haunted by sins that have been cast as far as the east is from the west.

> For as high as the heavens are above the earth,
>   so great is his love for those who fear him;
> as far as the east is from the west,
>   so far has he removed our transgressions from us.
> As a father has compassion on his children,
>   so the LORD has compassion on those who fear him.
>
> (PSALM 103:11-13)

These memories don't live in her past. They live in her now. They haunt her regularly like a spine-chilling horror film monster. And as much as she would like to move forward in forgiveness, she just can't find the courage to scare the monster away.

In the New Testament book of John, chapter 8, we meet a woman caught in the act of adultery. The legalistic teachers of the law and the Pharisees brought her before Jesus. They publicly humiliated her in front of all the townspeople, saying to Jesus, "Teacher, this woman was caught in the act of adultery. In the Law Moses commanded us to stone such women. Now what do you say?" (John 8:4-5).

Jesus bent down and wrote on the ground with his finger as they continued to question him. (This is one of those stories where I wish that Scripture revealed more information. What was Jesus writing? Was He doodling, or was He writing something significant like the Ten Commandments?) Finally, "He straightened up and said to them, 'If any one of you is without sin, let him be the first to throw a stone at her.' Again he stooped down and wrote on the ground" (John 8:7-8).

The crowd eventually thinned to nothing. The older, wiser men cleared first. Then the younger ones trickled away. When the adulterous woman and Jesus were the only ones remaining:

> Jesus straightened up and asked her, "Woman, where are they? Has no one condemned you?"
>
> "No one, sir," she said.
>
> "Then neither do I condemn you," Jesus declared. "Go now and leave your life of sin."
>
> (JOHN 8:10-12)

My sister, do you see that our holy Lord delights to show us mercy? He does not condemn us as we deserve. Time and time again, Scripture reveals merciful pictures of forgiveness. The woman in this story was guilty when she was brought to face Jesus, but as she left His presence, her guilt was forgiven. Her trash basket was empty.

When we turn to face Jesus with repentant hearts, our guilt is forgiven as well.

Toss Your Trash

This account of the adulterous woman teaches us a valuable lesson about judging and condemning others. We shouldn't do it. It's not appropriate and it's not our place. Simple as that.

But what does this lesson teach us about judging *ourselves?* My friend that I spoke of earlier carried around a trash basket filled with junk she threw in herself. Sure, it was accompanied by trash from other people too, but the lingering condemnation came from memories of decisions she had made, things she had done, places she had been, and brokenness she had experienced because of her own choices. In her heart, she accepts the forgiveness of Jesus, but she can't bear to forgive herself.

So many women won't forgive themselves.

I've been that woman.

I know that woman.

I know that self-loathing. I've lived it. I'm not going to tell you that forgiving yourself is easy. It's hard—and, in a lot of ways, it should be. But I can testify that it wasn't until I prayerfully allowed the stubborn, strong, and unconditional love of Jesus to pry my fingers off the lid of my trash basket and empty the condemning contents that I experienced true freedom and complete forgiveness.

Is there something that you have not been able to forgive yourself for?

Karl Menninger, the famed psychiatrist, once said that if he could convince the patients in psychiatric hospitals that their sins were forgiven, 75 percent of them could walk out the next day. If you have confessed your sins to the Lord, I beg you: Do not be held captive by guilt and shame any longer! A heart that is made right in the sight of the Lord is a heart that is worthy of forgiveness. Not worthy in itself, but worthy in Christ Jesus. "So if the Son sets you free, you will be free indeed" (John 8:36). The God-man, Jesus Christ, is the one who said that.

Does your heart know freedom, or are you like one of the psych patients imprisoned by guilt? There's an old saying: *Those with a clear conscious have a bad memory.* But that's not true for those of us who are forgiven through the blood of Christ.

My friend, we need to stop beating ourselves up for sins of our past. We need to stop allowing guilt and shame to chain us to unproductive living. Jesus humbled Himself by becoming human, endured an excruciating death, and then defied the grave in His resurrection so that we could be restored to a place of complete healing. *Complete* healing.

Second Corinthians 5:21 states that "God made Him who had no sin to be sin for us, so that in him we might become the righteousness of God." If you are in Christ, the Bible says that your guilt was paid for on the cross of Calvary. Jesus carried the sins of the world on *His* shoulders so that you wouldn't have to carry them on yours.

If you are holding on to unconfessed sin, the time has come for you to release your grip. God's Word promises that, "If we confess our sins, he is faithful and just and will forgive us our sins and purify us from all unrighteousness" (1 John 1:9).

Accept His forgiveness.

None of us is perfect, just perfectly forgiven. Take your hand off the lid and allow the Lord to empty your trash basket of every last condemning voice once and for all. Embrace the freedom that Jesus intends for you to live in.

A preacher of the early 1900s said that when he was twelve years old, he killed one of the family geese by throwing a stone and hitting it squarely on the head. He buried the dead fowl and figured his parents wouldn't notice that one of the twenty-four birds was missing. But that evening his sister called him aside and said, "I saw what you did. If you don't offer to do the dishes tonight, I'll tell Mother." The next morning she gave him the same warning. All that day and the next the frightened boy felt bound to do the dishes. The following morning, however, he surprised his sister by telling her it was her turn. When she quietly reminded him of what she could do, he said, "I've already told Mother, and she has forgiven me. Now you do the dishes. I'm free again!"

Embrace His Grace

We all struggle with sin simply because we are human.

> Everyone has turned away,
>   they have together become corrupt;

there is no one who does good,
   not even one.

(PSALM 53:3)

Let's be real here, we are saved by grace, not by our goodness. Grace is *unmerited* favor. Not deserved. Not earned.

I wrestle with sin all the time. My flesh loves to throw my spirit into a tizzy. But I know I'm not alone, and neither are you. The apostle Paul was one of the most passionate men of Christ who ever walked the earth, and even he struggled daily.

> I know that nothing good lives in me, that is, in my sinful nature. For I have the desire to do what is good, but I cannot carry it out. For what I do is not the good I want to do; no, the evil I do not want to do—this I keep on doing. Now if I do what I do not want to do, it is no longer I who do it, but it is sin living in me that does it (Romans 7:18-20).

I sat in the dentist chair recently and considered the state of my teeth. Even though I brush two times a day, stains are still a problem. I hate that. I like my teeth to sparkle. I want them to rank "fabulously white" on the sliding scale of teeth colors.

I'm sure my two cups of coffee each morning don't help, but for goodness' sake, I take care of my teeth! I use whitening toothpaste with fluoride, brush in circles for two minutes or more, and I floss. (Okay, so I don't floss every day...but I do floss.) In spite of my efforts, I still have to visit my dentist every six months for a good cleaning.

It occurs to me that stains probably build up in our hearts over time, too. It's a gradual thing. Even if we confess our sins daily, I believe we can still encounter residual buildup of unholiness. Now hear me, friend, this is not a message of condemnation. I live freely in the promise found in Romans 8:1, "Therefore, there is now no condemnation for those who are in Christ Jesus." I trust that our Lord forgives and forgets our confessed sins completely. But we need to be careful. Subtle choices such as resentment, laziness, gossip, selfishness, unforgiveness, self-indulgence, pride, and uncontrolled anger (among other things) can diminish the shine on our souls and keep us from God's best.

It's time for a good cleaning. God wants you to cast aside everything that keeps you from Him. As you invite God to change your heart, the laser treatment of His holy light will remove lingering stains that dull the appearance and evidences of your faith and purity. When you sincerely turn your heart toward God, He will remove any stains that have built up on your soul.

> Those who look on him are radiant;
> their faces are never covered with shame.
>
> (PSALM 34:5)

A Sinful Woman Is Forgiven

Luke 7 introduces us to a woman who endured her shame publicly. *Radiant* was surely not a word she would use to describe herself. She was guilty of something, though we are never told what. She is simply described as a woman "who had lived a sinful life." Though she is nameless to you and me, the people of her town surely knew her name. The Pharisees knew enough to condemn her with judgmental thoughts. I wouldn't be surprised if the women in her town condemned her with social isolation or perhaps with disapproving stares. Maybe they shunned her with silence. Or attacked her with gossip.

Her sin was public, not private. Yet the public disgrace of this broken, sinful woman became the perfect canvas for Jesus Christ to paint a beautiful picture of extravagant grace.

> Now one of the Pharisees invited Jesus to have dinner with him, so he went to the Pharisee's house and reclined at the table. When a woman who had lived a sinful life in that town learned that Jesus was eating at the Pharisee's house, she brought an alabaster jar of perfume, and as she stood behind him at his feet weeping, she began to wet his feet with her

tears. Then she wiped them with her hair, kissed them and poured perfume on them (Luke 7:36-38).

Imagine what a scandalous moment this must have been. I'm sure the host was wondering how this uninvited woman managed to get into his home. We know his mind was racing, because the next few verses tell us so:

> When the Pharisee who had invited him saw this, he said to himself, "If this man were a prophet, he would know who is touching him and what kind of woman she is—that she is a sinner."
>
> Jesus answered him, "Simon, I have something to tell you."
>
> "Tell me, teacher," he said.
>
> "Two men owed money to a certain moneylender. One owed him five hundred denarii, and the other fifty. Neither of them had the money to pay him back, so he canceled the debts of both. Now which of them will love him more?"
>
> Simon replied, "I suppose the one who had the bigger debt canceled."
>
> "You have judged correctly," Jesus said.
>
> Then he turned toward the woman and said to Simon, "Do you see this woman? I came into your house. You did not give me any water for my feet, but she wet my feet with her tears and wiped them with her hair. You did not give me a kiss, but this woman, from the time I entered, has not stopped kissing my feet. You did not put oil on my head, but she has poured perfume on my feet. Therefore, I tell you, her many sins have been forgiven—for she loved much. But he who has been forgiven little loves little."
>
> Then Jesus said to her, "Your sins are forgiven" (vv. 39-48).

Imagine the freedom that flooded this woman's soul when she looked up, through tear-filled eyes, into the face of grace for the very first time. Jesus looked beyond her reputation to her regret. Then He forgave her. Not because she had earned forgiveness, but because Jesus loved her.

She was forgiven much, so she loved Him much. Oh, how I can relate to this sinful woman. The love that resides in my heart is so great because the sins I've been forgiven of are so many.

> Amazing grace—how sweet the sound—
> That saved a wretch like me!
> I once was lost but now am found,
> Was blind, but now I see.

Jesus still loves to extend grace, and I am so thankful. Grace! What none of us deserves, but each of us longs for. Philip Yancey, in his book *What's So Amazing About Grace?*, wrote:

> Grace does not excuse sin, but it treasures the sinner. True grace is shocking, scandalous. It shakes our conventions with its insistence on getting close to sinners and touching them with mercy and hope. It forgives the unfaithful spouse, the racist, the child abuser. It loves today's AIDS-ridden addict as much as the tax collector of Jesus' day.

God created us to know Him, to love Him, and to respond to Him. From the beginning, His desire has always been to be loved by His creation. Jesus said that the most important thing you could ever do is, " 'Love the Lord your God with all your heart and with all your soul and with all your mind' " (Matthew 22:37). God desires to be the center of your attention, to have a meaningful and satisfying relationship with you.

In his book *3:16, The Numbers of Hope,* Max Lucado writes, "The heart of the human problem is the heart of the human. And God's treatment is prescribed in John 3:16." It's the verse you've more than likely heard since you were a child. The verse that is scribbled on cardboard signs and held up at sporting events. The verse that gives hope to each and every one of us: "For God so loved the world that he gave his one and only Son, that whoever believes in him shall not perish but have eternal life" (John 3:16).

His death was the great exchange. Jesus, who was perfectly beautiful in heaven, came to earth, became a man, and lived a sinless life. He took on the sins of the world as He submitted to death on a cross. But death couldn't hold Him! He rose again on the third day. All for one life-changing reason: so that we, who are broken, could become perfectly beautiful by placing our faith in Him.

Why would He lay down His life for you, for me, and for all humanity? In one word: love. Perfect, unconditional, doesn't-matter-who-you-are-or-where-you've-been-or-what-you've-done love. God made a new and living way through the blood of Jesus Christ so our wounded hearts could be restored.

Sara's Slippery Slope

Sara knows well the contrast of guilt and forgiveness. There was a time when guilt from sin almost suffocated her faith. Choices she made led her off the well-lit, straight and narrow path, down some very dark, curvy alleys.

Sara was raised in a loving, Christian home. She grew up attending church and prayed to receive Jesus as her Savior at a young age. But as a teenager, Sara lost interest in her childhood conversion. She set aside faith for a season.

Sara was popular with other high school students. With thick, chestnut hair and big brown eyes, Sara's physical beauty demanded that others take note of her. She was a good girl by the world's standards. Likable. She got excellent grades and served on student counsel and as a class officer. Yet, in spite of appearances, Sara lacked confidence and felt incomplete.

Desperate to feel valued, and thinking that satisfaction could be found in the arms of another, as a teenager she surrendered her innocence to promiscuity. Throughout high school and college, Sara always had a boyfriend. Believing that relationships were the drink that her soul thirsted for, Sara really tried to make them work. To her, sex became a natural part of each relationship. She didn't feel like she was "sleeping around," because she was *in love with* and *monogamous with* each long-term boyfriend.

God began to draw Sara back to His heart toward the end of her college days. While she was excited to reconnect with her heavenly Father, the sexual relationship she had with her boyfriend became a barrier to complete intimacy with God. She rationalized her behavior and resisted complete surrender to God's ways. So for a long time Sara danced the spiritual hokey pokey with God…one foot in and one foot out.

Sara wanted God in her life, but on her terms. More than landing a fabulous job after graduation, she wanted her finger to be decorated with a diamond. She had plans for her life, and one major plan was to be married.

She wanted the happily ever after.

When graduation came and went with no engagement, Sara allowed seeds of resentment to take root in her heart. She was angry with God. She felt as if her prayers were invisible to this all-seeing God. The plans she had for her life were getting all messed up, and it frustrated her to no end.

The next ten years were a rollercoaster of spiritual highs and lows. At times Sara thrived in faith, Bible study, and church fellowship. At other times her interest waned, and she got distracted and experienced little joy. She moved from city to city and changed jobs several times. No place seemed like home. No relationship seemed like "the one." And her life was just not what she thought it should be.

At the age of thirty-five, she was still single. Although her Black-Berry boasted an exotic corporate travel schedule, Sara constantly wrestled with feeling unwanted as a woman. "Always the bridesmaid and never the bride" became a hated phrase. As a successful business-woman, she walked with a confident spring in her step, but inwardly, Sara walked with a limp.

About this time, Sara's brother and his wife welcomed a baby girl into the world. This little angel was the first grandchild for Sara's parents and a ray of light to their family. Sara loved being an aunt and loved her niece the instant she laid eyes on her.

Sadly, all the love in the world couldn't save her niece's life. She had been born with a defective heart, and surgery after fruitless surgery came and went. Prayer after seemingly fruitless prayer went up to God. Why was He allowing this to happen? This baby was innocent! The ordeal left Sara and her family spiritually exhausted and emotionally crushed. They buried this precious child at just nine months old.

The Costly Comfort Chase

Sara and her family struggled to understand and accept their tragic loss. Sara became numb to both life and faith. She felt as though she was in a fight to survive. Life had landed one blow after another right on her chin. While faith shielded her from complete hopelessness, discouragement kept beating her up.

She had finally had it with God.

She was angry. God had not saved her niece, and He certainly didn't seem concerned about bringing her a husband. Bitterness began to eat away at Sara's heart.

That bitterness fueled rebellion. Sara was just plumb tired of disappointment, so she turned from her convictions and defiantly went on a mission to ease her pain in an old, familiar way. Sara found "comfort" in the arms of a man. But this time, he was a married man.

Business trips became the backdrop for infidelity with her lover. When she was with him, she secretly pretended to be his wife. Like the prodigal son in Luke 15 who "set off for a distant country and there squandered his wealth in wild living" (v. 13), Sara left God and compromised her faith for another season. She ran hard and fast hoping to find something that would cover up the pain and bitterness and drown out the conviction of the Holy Spirit in her heart.

Let's pause here to look at the rest of the parable of the prodigal, and then we will return to Sara.

"After he had spent everything, there was a severe famine in that whole country, and he began to be in need. So he went and hired himself out to a citizen of that country, who sent him to his fields to feed pigs. He longed to fill his stomach with the pods that the pigs were eating, but no one gave him anything.

"*When he came to his senses,* he said, 'How many of my father's hired men have food to spare, and here I am starving to death! I will set out and go back to my father and say to him: Father, I have sinned against heaven and against you. I am no longer worthy to be called your son; make me like one of your hired men.' So he got up and went to his father" (Luke 15:14-20, emphasis mine).

Did you catch that phrase? "When he came to his senses." How many times have you and I been caught up in the lies of this world, only to later come to our senses? I shudder to think of the number of times I've been there.

"But while he was still a long way off, his father saw him and was filled with compassion for him; he ran to his son, threw his arms around him and kissed him.

"The son said to him, 'Father, I have sinned against heaven and against you. I am no longer worthy to be called your son.'

"But the father said to his servants, 'Quick! Bring the best robe and put it on him. Put a ring on his finger and sandals on his feet. Bring the fattened calf and kill it. Let's have a feast and celebrate. For this son of mine was dead and is alive again; he was lost and is found.' So they began to celebrate" (vv. 20-24).

A sinful child had come home and a celebration took place! There would be no condemnation from the father because his son came to him with a repentant heart. Mercy was shown and love was given lavishly to this undeserving lost one.

What Was Lost Is Found

Sara's story takes a similar turn here.

Though for a sliver of time the affair fueled her fantasy of being married, the relationship didn't cover up any of her pain. It left her more miserable than ever. She knew it was wrong. She hated who she had become. What she thought would be a relationship that could meet her needs as a woman caused her to be even more needy. Even more deprived.

Starved to death, you might say.

But turning back wasn't easy for Sara. The enemy tried to tell her that she had gone too far from home. There could be no turning back for her. Guilt and shame held her captive. Condemnation shouted to her mind, *You've messed up too much this time! You're no longer a Christian. God would never want someone like you.* At the same time, the Holy Spirit whispered to her soul, "You are God's daughter. He's waiting for you to come home. Turn back! He loves you!"

When she came to her senses, Sara turned toward home and ended the affair.

She went to her Father and cried, "I have sinned against heaven and I have sinned against you. I'm not worthy to be called your daughter. Please forgive me." And in a celestial instant, her wounded heart was restored. A heavenly party took place because a precious daughter who had been lost was now found (Luke 15:3-7).

It's been several years since Sara's affair with that married man. While it was difficult at first, she has chosen to forgive herself. Guilt no longer holds her captive. She is active in church, growing in her faith, and thriving in the freedom of forgiveness.

God loves us unconditionally. His love is available to each wandering heart. It doesn't matter if you've wandered just a few yards from Him or if you've ventured far away. It's never too late to turn back to God.

That's truth. Believe it.

God is waiting with open arms for all prodigal children to come home. When He sees a lost child turn toward home, He doesn't stand there with hands on His waist and an angry, you-should-be-ashamed-of-yourself look. He *runs* to her with arms wide open! You are His precious daughter, loved and chosen.

I hope you know without a doubt that God loves you completely. Unconditionally. He looks past your past to forgiveness.

Do you need to turn toward Him today? Have you left home? Have you squandered your days on wild living? Have sinful patterns built a barrier between the Lord and you? Whether you've gone far away or just a few rebellious, stubborn steps away—turn back now.

> Therefore, brothers, since we have confidence to enter the Most Holy Place by the blood of Jesus, by a new and living way opened for us through the curtain, that is, his body, and since we have a great priest over the house of God, let us draw near to God with a sincere heart in full assurance of faith, having our hearts sprinkled to cleanse us from a guilty conscience and having our bodies washed with pure water (Hebrews 10:19-22).

"Through the Veil"
Words and music by Gwen Smith

Through the veil, there's a new and living way
Through the curtain, welcome to the Holy Place
Though we once were separated
We are now invited in
Through the veil, through the blood, come to Him
Through the veil, through the blood, enter in

The Holy Place is open, come and worship
The Lamb for Sinners slain is King of all
We praise and glorify the Lord before His mighty throne
Through the veil, through the blood, come to Him
Through the veil, through the blood, enter in

4

Hungry into Satisfied

Satisfy us in the morning with your unfailing love,
that we may sing for joy and be glad all our days.

PSALM 90:14

One night as Brad and I prepared to put our kids to bed, our middle child, Hunter, had an emotional meltdown. Our little gumdrop went from sweet to sour in two seconds flat. The day had been packed full with school and other activities, and it was late. He should have turned into a pumpkin a smidgen before his meltdown took place. You know how those days are.

In an eight-year-old kind of way, Hunter was completely irrational. Tears flowed freely as he floated down his raging river of drama. He said that nobody loved him and that he felt mistreated. I had to just shake my head and wonder, "How in the world could one of my children feel unloved?"

The love Brad and I have for our children is immovable-mountain strong. We are not perfect, nor do we love them perfectly, but we do tell them of our love daily with words. We show them through our actions. We hug and affirm. We laugh and play with them. We spend our lives loving our children. It amazes me that any of our children could think, for even one second, that they are not loved.

As we endured the tear-filled bedtime drama, Brad and I suddenly realized why our son had such a dim perspective: he was hungry. Really hungry.

Earlier that evening, Hunter had chosen not to finish his dinner.

Our son believes he should have choices. We assure him that he *does* have choices—eat or be hungry. Simple as that.

A Satisfied Soul

As I emptied the dishwasher this morning, it occurred to me that we were created to be hungry. Our bodies need constant nourishment, and hunger is simply a trigger designed by God to stimulate a necessary response. Whether we're talking about physical, emotional, mental, or spiritual hunger, you and I are temporarily satisfied when an appropriate response meets a need.

Think about it…

The satisfying response to physical hunger is food and drink.

The satisfying response to emotional hunger is love (among other things).

The satisfying response to mental hunger is knowledge.

And the *only* satisfying response to spiritual hunger is God. Nothing can take His place. Not the latest-greatest beauty gimmick, not the most fabulous outfit, not a hunky man or a good smelling baby. Not money in the bank, not that promotion you might be after, not the affection you might be craving, and not the appreciation you desire for your efforts. Nothing can supplant God if you want to satisfy your spiritual hunger.

Constant Cravings

Our souls constantly demand to be fed, and make no mistake about it: if God does not have the proper place in your life, your soul will remain hungry. When I invite God into my days, I experience His satisfying presence no matter what I face. But when I don't pray, when I don't read my Bible, and when I don't praise, I get hungry. Really hungry (not to mention grouchy).

Christians are hungry people. Just like the Israelites who wandered in the desert, we need God's daily bread, His spiritual manna. Jesus taught us to ask for a *daily* portion. In the New Testament book of Matthew, Jesus took a moment to teach His followers how to pray. In that prayer, commonly referred to as the Lord's Prayer, He said, "Give us today our *daily* bread" (Matthew 6:11).

He didn't ask to be fed for an entire week—just for today.

We would be wise to do the same.

Some people might think that once we become Christians all of our spiritual hunger subsides. Not so! I've found that the more I get to know God, the more I *want* to know Him. The more I experience His peace, presence, and power in my life, the more I *want* to experience His peace, presence, and power. I crave Him more.

In John 4:13, Jesus says to a Samaritan woman at Jacob's well, " 'Everyone who drinks this water will be thirsty again.' " He was referring to the water in the well and a body's physical thirst. But then He tells her what He can offer her soul: " 'but whoever drinks the water I give him will never thirst. Indeed, the water I give him will become in him a spring of water welling up to eternal life' " (v. 14).

Jesus also addressed spiritual thirst and hunger when He spoke to a large crowd outside Capernaum. The day before, He had met their physical need by miraculously feeding over five thousand hungry people on a hill near the Sea of Galilee. But on this day, the crowds questioned Him about what God wanted them to do. Jesus told them that they must " 'believe in the one [God] has sent' " (John 6:29). (God isn't satisfied by what we do, but by *whom* we believe.) From there, the conversation went like this:

> So they asked him, "What miraculous sign then will you give that we may see it and believe you? What will you do? Our forefathers ate the manna in the desert; as it is written: 'He gave them bread from heaven to eat.' "
>
> Jesus said to them, "I tell you the truth, it is not Moses who has given you the bread from heaven, but it is my Father who gives you the true bread from heaven. For the bread of God is he who comes down from heaven and gives life to the world."
>
> "Sir," they said, "from now on give us this bread."

Then Jesus declared, "I am the bread of life. He who comes to me will never go hungry, and he who believes in me will never be thirsty" (John 6:30-35).

Every day we eat bread (food) to keep us healthy and strong. We stay healthy and strong spiritually by continually communing with Jesus. He calls Himself the Bread of Life as well as the Living Water. In order for food and water to sustain and strengthen us physically, we must eat and drink it. Likewise, we need to call on Jesus each day to sustain us spiritually.

Quench Your Thirst

A friend of mine is hypoglycemic. Before he was diagnosed, he had one compelling symptom. He was constantly thirsty. The crazy thing was, the more water he drank, the thirstier he became. It defies logic. As you live out your faith, you will have a similar insatiable thirst and hunger for God. The more you ask for His daily help, the more you will want it. But know this, friend, you will not be fully satisfied or quenched until you are in His presence.

In his book, *Come Thirsty,* Max Lucado writes:

> You're acquainted with physical thirst. Stop drinking and see what happens. Coherent thoughts vanish, skin grows clammy, and vital organs shut down. Deprive your body of necessary fluid, and it will tell you.
>
> Deprive your soul of spiritual water, and it will tell you. Dehydrated hearts send desperate messages. Snarling tempers. Waves of worry. Growing guilt and fear. Hopelessness. Resentment. Loneliness. Insecurity.
>
> But you don't have to live with a dehydrated heart. God invites you to treat your thirsty soul as you would treat your physical thirst. Just visit the WELL and drink deeply.

Here on earth, hunger and thirst never end. Just because you ate breakfast this morning doesn't mean you won't have a grumbly tummy at lunchtime. And when you eat lunch, that doesn't cover you for the next three days. You need to eat again and again.

The spiritual parallels here are as rich as a piece of Ghirardelli cheesecake from the Cheesecake Factory. (Great restaurant, by the way.) A three-course meal of worship, prayer, and a sermon on Sunday morning doesn't nourish your body with the spiritual calories you need for an entire week. Not by a long stretch. We were designed in the image of God, for God. We were made to worship. To respond to the glory of God. To know Him. Continually. Daily. Without ceasing.

I don't know about you, but hunger affects my judgment. If I dare go to the grocery store while I'm hungry, my cart will usually contain extra food items I wouldn't normally purchase. Are you smellin' what I'm cookin' here? If I'm hungry when I arrive at a dinner party, I'll more than likely eat the mother lode of appetizers (especially if there is dip involved).

When we are spiritually hungry, the same truth applies. We have a tendency to compromise our judgment and set aside our convictions. We grumble and complain about our lives. We look to other people and other stuff to meet our needs.

Being Spiritually Thin Is Not In!

Look around! Spiritually hungry people are everywhere. Just turn on your television, pick up a magazine, or go to an online chat room. People are desperately trying to fill their hunger hole...trying to find happiness and satisfaction in things, status, and people.

Now, if you dare, look even closer to home. Look at your PTA meetings, boardrooms, Little League fields, and malls. And if you're really brave, look in the mirror. Each one of us sees a hungry woman staring us in the face.

It is really important to turn to the Bread of Life at the first inkling of hunger pangs. Go to Him with your needs and give Him your burdens. Jesus said: "Come to me, all you who are weary and burdened, and I will give you rest" (Matthew 11:28). He wants to meet you at the point of your need.

God gave you an open invitation to come to Him when He said through the prophet Isaiah,

> "Come, all who are thirsty,
>   come to the waters;
> and you who have no money,
>   come, buy and eat!"
>
> (Isaiah 55:1A)

Each time we connect with God throughout the day, our souls are nourished. Sometimes we just need a small spiritual meal. Sometimes our needs are greater. In those moments, we are invited by our compassionate God to sit down to a great big dinner.

A small meal might be when you read a Bible passage and prayerfully ask God to reveal His truth and application of that Scripture. He loves when we seek Him in Scripture! In the book of Jeremiah, God said that if we seek Him, we will find Him if we search for Him with all our heart (29:13). Spending time with the Lord through His Word is one great way to feed your soul.

Do you remember in grade school learning about the food pyramid? The following spiritual disciplines are the building blocks of what I like to call the Faith Food Pyramid. Just like a nutritional food pyramid that encourages us to eat a recommended daily allowance of fruits, vegetables, meats, and grains, the Faith Food Pyramid shows the essential nutrients for a well-nourished soul. Our souls are fed when we experience God each day through the basic faith food groups:

1. Praying
2. Reading the Bible
3. Worshiping

Do you set aside time each day to pray, read the Bible, and respond to God in worship? This is basic faith food stuff. No secrets here. No fad spiritual diet. Nothing fancy or lacy, just the basics.

Faith Food Basics

Now, some people like to snack, and I'm one of them. A snack is an afternoon necessity for me. Come 3:00 p.m., my body aches for a little somethin'-somethin'. A spiritual snack can also hit the spot in the middle of a long day. Some of my favorite spiritual snacks are: Scripture verses, worship music, Christian radio, devotionals, and Christian magazines or books. Whether you spend three minutes snacking or thirty, snacks should never replace your main meals.

God wants you to live a full life, regardless of the trials you face. Satan wants you to remain wanting. He wants you to experience a constant, insatiable hunger, but he wants you to try to satisfy that hunger with empty, hamster-wheel living where you constantly run but never get anywhere. Jesus said in John 10:10 that "the thief comes only to steal and kill and destroy; I have come that they may have life, and have it to the full."

Funny though, I've known about these faith food basics for as long as I've been a Christian (I'd venture to guess that you have too), but there are still so many days I rob my soul of a good meal. And, as I said earlier, when I'm hungry I don't always make the best decisions.

Another negative consequence of spiritual hunger is that I often feel discontent. Discontent with what? You name it—my husband, my kids, my house, my hair, my weight, my looks, my job, my abilities, my this, and my that. Spiritual hunger in my life isn't always subtle. Sometimes my deficiencies are as obvious as the mole on Cindy Crawford's face. Without even realizing it, my ability to love, show patience, extend grace, and walk in wisdom can fade. When hunger seeps into my soul, I also have a strong tendency to become ungrateful.

In Psalm 107:8-9, the psalmist wrote,

> Let them give thanks to the LORD for his unfailing love
>   and his wonderful deeds for men,
> for he satisfies the thirsty
>   and fills the hungry with good things.

Why do we allow ourselves to become spiritually hungry?

God loves us and He loves to feed our souls. Yet, in spite of all evidence, sometimes we don't *feel* loved by God. And when we don't feel loved, we ladies have a tendency to grumble and whine. Nothing illuminates my lamentations like a grumbly spiritual tummy. It's dangerous for us to allow emotions to drive our faith. We've already concluded that hunger affects our judgment, so it's important that we be vigilant in defending our souls against hunger.

Danita's Portion

While much of the spiritual hunger we feel is a result of us not turning to God, sometimes we get pangs of hunger for other reasons. Often pressure and stress can increase the awareness of our need for God.

Danita is a Christian who experienced a tragic loss. Though her faith was strong, she found herself needing an even greater portion from God when loss came her way. As she walked through the valley of the shadow of death, her pangs of spiritual hunger were satisfied in God's compassionate love.

Let me tell you her story.

Danita lived the dream. She had a strong faith, a beautiful tropical island home, and a loving husband named Dave.

Dave was a military officer stationed at Pearl Harbor in Hawaii. An avid runner, he was the picture of fitness and good health. At six feet, one inch tall, his tanned, athletic build never failed to take Danita's breath away. Especially when he wore his "Officer and a Gentleman" dress whites.

As handsome as he was, one of Dave's most charming qualities was his sense of humor. The man could throw down some serious funny. The kind of funny that could render Danita defenseless, smack-dab in the middle of an argument.

Like every other couple, they had their issues. But they worked hard on their marriage and strived to live together as one. Early on they had surrendered their household to the Lord and continually sought His leading. Faith, friendship, and fun were the foundations of their home and the cement that held them together during difficult times.

Dave and Danita made time for each other. They traveled, watched sports on TV, played cards, went to movies, and relaxed on the beach together.

They had made it past many painful years of fruitless infertility treatments. Through God's help, they eventually conceived and delivered their first child, a beautiful baby girl named Kelsey. Years later they were blessed to adopt another precious child, a daughter named Audrey.

It was a beautiful life.

Both Danita and Dave were committed Christians who desired for God to be glorified through them. They were people of faith who prayed regularly, sought God's leading, and tried their hardest to live out His purpose for their lives.

The Last Good-bye

In October 2003, after returning home from their Wednesday night church service, Dave and Danita tucked their daughters in bed and then sat down to discuss their future. Dave had been wrestling with some issues of spiritual surrender about the possible relocation of their family. (In the military, officers are eligible for new orders every three years, and their time was due.) God had really got ahold of Dave's heart during worship that evening, and he couldn't wait to tell Danita about it. When they sat down, he told her that he had finally turned the details of his new orders over completely to God. He decided that he would no longer cling to control. He had slipped the fuzzy details of his future into the Lord's hands and was finally at peace.

The next morning, Dave woke before the sun and began his morning routine while Danita slept. Just before he left to go to work, Dave turned on the coffee machine and tenderly kissed Danita. As their lips met, he whispered, "Goodbye. I love you, babe," then walked out the door.

If only Danita had known that would be their last kiss! She would have pulled him close, held him tight, and gazed into his amazing blue eyes. She would've taken a long, deep breath to fill her senses with the aroma of his cologne. She would've drunk in his presence and savored his warmth. She would have told him that she loved being his wife and was ready for their next great adventure together.

My Lips Will Glorify

When the phone rang at 7:30 a.m., Danita was startled. It seemed a bit early for the phone to start ringing. A secretary from the naval base said, "Dave has collapsed! The military EMS have been called, and we need you to meet them at the hospital!" The words pierced Danita's heart.

The drive to the hospital was quick. She ran inside the emergency room, only to find that the ambulance had not arrived yet. As she hurried back to the parking lot, a passage of Scripture flooded her mind. Danita began to speak it out loud:

> O God, you are my God,
>> earnestly I seek you;
> my soul thirsts for you,
>> my body longs for you,
> in a dry and weary land
>> where there is no water.
> I have seen you in the sanctuary
>> and beheld your power and glory.
> Because your love is better than life,
>> my lips will glorify you.
> I will praise you as long as I live,
>> and in your name I will lift up my hands.
> My soul will be satisfied as with the richest of foods;
>> with singing lips my mouth will praise you.
> On my bed I remember you;
>> I think of you through the watches of the night.

Because you are my help,
I sing in the shadow of your wings.
My soul clings to you;
your right hand upholds me.

(PSALM 63:1-8)

As soon as she spoke the words, "Because your love is better than life, my lips will glorify you," Danita knew in her heart Dave was gone. Her soul felt it.

Minutes later, a screaming siren announced the arrival of the ambulance. As the medics ushered Dave into the emergency room and worked feverishly to resuscitate him, Danita rushed to be by his side. An emergency room nurse pulled her away and insisted that she sit in the waiting room.

Friends began to arrive, but Danita couldn't speak to anyone. Words just weren't an option. She sat silently, as every fiber of her being screamed, *This can't be happening! Dave is a rock. He's a healthy man. He's too young to die! Lord, please don't let him die!*

Before long, Danita was called to the back where an emergency room doctor told her that Dave had died. The weight of those words hit her with the impact of a bullet shot at pointblank range.

It couldn't be true.

It just couldn't be.

She asked her best friend to come back with her to the room where Dave had just been pronounced dead. It was a surreal moment. Danita spoke to her husband through shaky sobs as his body lay lifeless. She touched his skin. The warmth was gone. She kissed him on the cheek and held his hand one last time. Dave was with the Lord now.

After signing some paperwork, Danita and her girlfriend headed back to the waiting room where more than thirty people had gathered. She saw her pastor in the crowd and asked if he could pray. They all bowed their heads and came around Danita in support. Her pastor prayed, then finished with the Twenty-third Psalm.

The LORD is my Shepherd, I shall not be in want.
　　He makes me lie down in green pastures,
he leads me beside quiet waters,
　　　he restores my soul.
He guides me in the paths of righteousness
　　　for his name's sake.
Even though I walk
　　　through the valley of the shadow of death,
I will fear no evil,
　　　for you are with me;
your rod and your staff,
　　　they comfort me.
You prepare a table before me
　　　in the presence of my enemies.
You anoint my head with oil;
　　　my cup overflows.
Surely goodness and love will follow me
　　　all the days of my life,
And I will dwell in the house of the LORD
　　　forever.

After they prayed, Danita needed to go. She needed fresh air. She needed to think. She needed to pray. She needed to wail.

It all seemed so crazy. She had arrived at the hospital a happily married woman and was leaving a heartbroken widow. She navigated through the foggy crowd of supportive friends, made her way to her car, and headed home.

The Lord Answers

The drive home was almost too much for Danita to bear. The sun shone brightly as she passed cars with surfboards on the roof. A long line of thirsty customers idled at the Starbucks drive-through. People all around her were going on at the speed of life while her life stood still.

She went home and headed straight to her bedroom. She cried out to God, "How will I tell Kelsey that she will never see her daddy again?

What will I say?" And He answered her. A devotional she had been reading the night before lay open on the bedside table. Highlighted on the page were the words of Psalm 16:

> LORD, you have assigned me my portion and my cup;
>> you have made my lot secure.
> The boundary lines have fallen for me in pleasant places;
>> surely I have a delightful inheritance.
> I will praise the LORD, who counsels me;
>> even at night my heart instructs me.
> I have set the LORD always before me.
>> Because he is at my right hand,
>> I will not be shaken.
> Therefore my heart is glad and my tongue rejoices;
>> my body also will rest secure,
> because you will not abandon me to the grave,
>> nor will you let your Holy One see decay.
> You have made known to me the path of life;
>> you will fill me with joy in your presence,
>> with eternal pleasures at your right hand.
>
>> (PSALM 16:5-11)

As devastating as Dave's death was, there was something special about the security her soul felt as she sobbed in anguish. God's Word attended to her desperate hunger. A strange peace embraced her. She felt safe. In spite of the circumstances, her soul was oddly satisfied. She was not alone. She knew her Lord had not abandoned her.

He was with her on the bed as she cried.

He was with her on the wood floor when she fell to weep.

He was with her in this very broken time.

Since Dave's funeral, Danita's journey from broken into beautiful has been challenging yet eternally rewarding. It's a journey she is still walking day by day, and like all of us, she has good days and bad.

Danita's appetite for God's provision of her daily portion has sky-rocketed. She's never known a greater need for God's strength to come alongside her weakness. For His hope to come alongside her despair. For His peace to replace her fears.

Ordinary tasks can easily throw her. She never would have thought that filling out a simple form could cause her heart to feel such an intense longing. For fifteen years she checked the box that said "married"; now she has to check the box that says "widowed."

Through it all, Danita has felt the far-reaching, compassionate, and loving arms of God embrace her in every painful moment. He comforted her each time she cried out to Him in the numbness of despair. She testifies, "We are all on a journey and there is no guarantee in life. There is not always a miracle. But God wants us to always trust that He has given us our portion. He will make the boundaries set for each of us."

Danita strongly believes that she is alive to do what God has called her to do: to testify of His amazing, never-leave-your-side love. God's love continues to transform her brokenness and satisfy her hungry soul.

Another Hungry Woman

In 1 Kings 17, we meet another widow. This widow was from a small village on the Mediterranean coast in Phoenicia called Zarephath of Sidon. We never learn her name, we don't know how old she was, and we never hear anything about her deceased husband.

That frustrates me a little bit. I want details! I want to hear how she and her husband met and got engaged. I'd love to hear about their wedding day and about their relationship. Did they get along and enjoy life together, or did they just exist in a loveless marriage?

I wonder if her husband was a boy from their village who used to tease her. Maybe they played tag in the marketplace with the other children of Zarephath. Or perhaps theirs had been an arranged marriage. Many of them were back then. Maybe she didn't know him at all until he began to court her.

And we don't know *how,* and we don't know *why* he died. His death could've been the result of a long-term sickness. It could've been a sudden heart attack or aneurism. It could've been an accident at work or an injury on the battlefield. I wonder if she was by her husband's side as he took his last breath. There's so much we don't know. But when it comes to the widow of Zarephath, we *do* know:

- Her husband died.
- She knew and listened to God.
- She was left to raise her son alone.
- She and her son were about to run out of food and were at the end of their hope rope.

My heart breaks just thinking about the pain she must have gone through. Though we are given few details, we know she was a woman familiar with pain and loss.

A woman much like you and me.

She was a woman with hopes and dreams. A woman with needs, wants, and desires. A wife who wanted to be loved and cared for by her husband. A mom who wanted her son to mind his manners, to honor her, and to show courtesy to others. She probably loved to laugh and to visit with friends over a cup of coffee. And like most married women, she probably anticipated growing old with her husband.

But life dealt her a different hand.

When we meet her in verse 10, she is searching for sticks to make a fire so she can go home and prepare a final meal for herself and her son. Why a final meal? There was a drought and famine in the land, and her supply of flour and oil was nearly exhausted.

Given this bleak situation, I can only imagine what she must have thought when God directed her to supply His prophet, Elijah, with food. The circumstances that she and her son faced seemed hopeless. How could she possibly feed someone else too? Though caught between faith and a hard place, she responded admirably. Her response is a wonderful model for us: she prayed, listened, and obeyed.

When I'm cornered by difficult circumstances, a part of me always wants to be in control. When I feel desperate, angry, empty, unnecessary, or helpless, it's not uncommon for me to try to figure out on my own how I can make things work.

Do you ever do that?

Remember this model: Pray—Listen—Obey.

Are you wondering how we know that the widow prayed? I'll address that in just a minute. But let me back up a few steps first.

Prior to being sent to Zarephath, Elijah, a prophet of God, had been residing in a wilderness area called the Kerith Ravine. While there, God provided for him daily. "The ravens brought him bread and meat in the morning and bread and meat in the evening, and he drank from the brook" (1 Kings 17:6).

When the brook eventually dried up, God told Elijah, " 'Go at once to Zarephath of Sidon and stay there. I have commanded a widow in that place to supply you with food'" (v. 9).

We can assume from the preceding text that our widow friend was a praying woman who knew the Lord. Not only did she pray to God, she listened to God. Perhaps she was expecting Elijah that day as she gathered sticks. This was a woman of faith who had learned to hear and discern the voice of God. A hungry woman of faith.

Not only was she physically hungry, she was also in a desperate situation. This was life or death, and she was without hope. But God saw her. He heard her cries. Here's the account of what happened once Elijah came to town:

> So he went to Zarephath. When he came to the town gate, a widow was there gathering sticks. He called to her and asked, "Would you bring me a little water in a jar so I may have a drink?" As she was going to get it, he called, "And bring me, please, a piece of bread."
>
> "As surely as the LORD your God lives," she replied, "I don't have any bread—only a handful of flour in a jar and a little oil in a jug. I am gathering a few sticks to take home and make a meal for myself and my son, that we may eat it—and die."
>
> Elijah said to her, "Don't be afraid. Go home and do as you have said. But first make a small cake of bread for me from what you have and bring it to me, and then make something

for yourself and your son. For this is what the LORD, the God of Israel, says: 'The jar of flour will not be used up and the jug of oil will not run dry until the day the LORD gives rain on the land.'"

She went away and did as Elijah had told her. So there was food every day for Elijah and for the woman and her family. For the jar of flour was not used up and the jug of oil did not run dry, in keeping with the word of the LORD spoken by Elijah (vv. 10-16).

Her miracle came when she obeyed God, when she chose to surrender, in an act of obedience, what was precious and highly valuable to her. Might God be asking you to surrender something? Something precious and valuable? Maybe it's a hurt or disappointment that you've been holding on to. Perhaps it's a troubled relationship. Trust Him. His blessings, provision, and miracles follow obedience.

Jehovah-Jireh, Our Provider

God's provision was available to the widow each day, but in order to receive the miracle, she had to reach her hand into the flour bin and pour oil from the jar. His provision is available to you each day too; you just need to reach for it in faith and receive it.

Our tender heavenly Father took care of His hungry daughter with admirable chivalry. He was her Jehovah-Jireh, the Lord her provider. He was responsive to her needs. In a beautiful display of His extravagant love, God provided for her in both practical and supernatural ways. He went beyond her physical need of food to her spiritual need for Him. He is such a compassionate God! He does not forget his hungry children.

When you invite God into your circumstances, He will faithfully respond to your needs as well.

Taste and see that the LORD is good;
blessed is the man who takes refuge in him.

Fear the LORD, you his saints,
>   for those who fear him lack nothing.
The lions may grow weak and hungry,
>   but those who seek the LORD lack no good thing.

(PSALM 34:8-10)

Sometimes we become so desperate and consumed by hopelessness that we gather sticks for our last meal. In those moments, I like to recite that old saying: Stop telling God how big your mountain is and start telling your mountain how big your God is! God has not ceased providing for His children. The very same God who each day miraculously supplied the ingredients for this widow's bread recipe is the One who delights to provide for us.

He Knows Your Needs

Exodus 16 demonstrates a similar example of God's daily provision. Moses had led the Israelites through the Red Sea in an amazing display of God's power. Just days later, the desert wanderers became grumpy and fussy…as if they hadn't just witnessed an active and mighty God provide them an extraordinary deliverance! As soon as they began to experience a bit of discomfort, all their confidence in God's ability flew out the window.

Oh, how I can relate to those complaining Israelites. Far too many times I have been delivered from a trial, only to fret and whine as soon as the next complication came my way. Can I hear an "Amen!" from the amen choir? I am so thankful that God's love is not fickle like my faith.

Our loving Father is keenly aware of your circumstances and your needs. The Scriptures show us time and time again that God hears the cries of His children.

The righteous cry out, and the LORD hears them;
>   he delivers them from all their troubles.

(PSALM 34:17)

What are you hungry for today? God longs to be your portion, to meet your essential needs, to be strong in your weakness, and to satisfy your deepest hunger. C'mon...pull up a chair. Taste and see that the Lord is good! "Blessed are those who hunger and thirst for righteousness, for they will be filled" (Matthew 5:6).

"Fill Me"

Words and music by Gwen Smith

So many days I feel defeated
Worthless, empty, and depleted
Then you remind me that You love me
You provide when I am hungry
I'm hungry now, I'm hungry now

Lord, fill me
Satisfy me
You are welcome to consume all that I am
Lord, fill me
Move completely
Occupy my soul, unveil your sovereign plan
Lord, fill me

When I'm searching hard for your eyes
When my heart is open real wide
Your gentle Spirit runs right to me
And offers myriad of mercies
I'm searching now, I'm searching now

[Chorus]

Spirit of the living God fall fresh on me
Spirit of the living God fall fresh on me, fall fresh on me
Melt me, mold me, fill me, use me

[Chorus]

5

Empty into Full

"The thief comes only to steal and kill and destroy;
I have come that they may have life, and have it to the full."
JOHN 10:10

When I was a kid, our church always hosted a big Easter egg hunt as a community outreach event. It was so exciting. On the egg-hunt day, the children's pastor, Sunday school teachers, and volunteer church members roped off a large grassy field down below the church building to keep anxious little hands from prematurely gathering the brightly colored eggs and candies. Then they would instruct us kids to stand behind the rope until they blew the whistle and dropped the rope. I remember swells of anticipation sweeping through me as I stood shoulder to shoulder with the other egg-hunters behind the rope. We held empty baskets in our hands and great expectations in our hearts.

Without fail, each kid that came with an empty basket went home with a full basket and a happy heart. It was simple. It was sweet. It was a sure thing. No child was left behind. No child was forgotten. Everyone got a basket full of treats. Life was good.

How I wish that life was always so simple and sweet.

If only we could line up each morning behind the roped-off grassy field of life and race in to gather love, hope, and peace like Easter eggs. That would be nice. Perfectly beautiful, in fact. But life isn't always so sweet and "Leave-It-To-Beaver-ish." Sometimes it's downright messy. Broken. Dirty. Disappointing. Empty.

The journey to beautiful includes valleys of emptiness for each of us. Times when we long to be filled. To be whole. To be well. To be loved. Christians are not kept from pain. We have no biblical promise that we won't endure hardships. To the contrary, Scripture makes it clear that each of us *will* endure trials and pain. Jesus said, "'In this world you will have trouble. But take heart! I have overcome the world'" (John 16:33b). Every believer and nonbeliever alike must endure times of brokenness. The promise for the believer is that in the trial, God will "never leave you nor forsake you" (Joshua 1:5). You are never alone. Hold tight to that promise, friend.

Sometimes we are brought through a trial by God. At other times, we are brought to God through a trial. Can you think of a few valleys of emptiness you've had to walk through in your life? I've been through more than I care to remember.

The Empty Nest

Last fall, some friends of mine became empty nesters when their only child went off to college. In spite of the excitement they shared for their daughter's new adventure, sorrow blanketed their hearts. They missed her presence in their home. They missed her drama. Her hugs. Her laughter. The absence of her voice at the dinner table screamed loudly in their souls. The father said that the first time he stepped into his daughter's bedroom after she was gone, he was overwhelmed with sadness. "I never knew our house could hold so much empty," he said.

Sometimes our souls can hold a whole lot of empty. When relationships fail. When sickness comes. When depression sets in. When we feel unattractive, unloved, or unwanted. When doubt, fear, anxiety, anger, and insecurity consume our hearts, emptiness takes up grand amounts of space.

Full of Empty

Amanda knows this type of emptiness and has had her fill of broken living. She grew up in a dysfunctional household in the bluegrass state of Kentucky. From what Amanda remembers of her childhood, she says that "bad memories far outweigh the good ones." Her parents separated when she was quite young, and her house was filled with anger, raised voices, verbal attacks, and substance abuse. Amanda's house was full of empty.

Her father paid little attention to her. She didn't feel loved by her dad, she didn't feel welcomed in his presence, and she didn't feel important in his world. Her mom was a Christian who was lost in a bad marriage and lived most of her days in survival mode. She parented without much grace and did what she could to make sure that Amanda and her older brother, Erik, were seen but not heard when their father was around. Erik was not the Wally Cleaver kind of older brother...more like the Eddie Haskell kind. Not in a playful, goof-off way but in a mean-spirited way. Erik took great pleasure in teasing and tormenting Amanda. He often told her that she was fat, and he genuinely seemed not to like her or want to be near her.

The brokenness of her family made the contrasting, perfect love of God very attractive to Amanda. As a little girl, she accepted Jesus as her Savior and felt most at home when she was actually at church. So Amanda went to church every time she could.

Even though she found solace at church, the turmoil that filled her heart seemed endless. Sometimes Amanda's dad would go off on drunken rampages, and her mom would flee to the neighbors. In one instance, Amanda was taking a bath when her mom grabbed Erik and ran to the safety of the neighbor's home. When Amanda got out of the tub and dried off, no one was home.

> I got out of the tub and started looking for my mom and brother. I went from room to room, but they were nowhere to be found. So I went to my neighbors' house, and they were there. I asked my mom, "What's the matter with Dad?" and "Why didn't you tell me you were leaving?" Her response was, "We had to get out of the house. Your dad is drunk and I was afraid." I stood there feeling very unsafe and thought, *Well, what about me? You left me there!*

Amanda's father all but abandoned her and Erik after he and her mother separated and eventually divorced. His absence left Amanda feeling even more unloved, insignificant, and forgotten.

"I vaguely remember my dad coming around," Amanda recalls. "He was a Vietnam veteran who worked third shift for the government, and he struggled with a heavy addiction to drugs and alcohol." He also cheated on her mother with a woman from work from the time Amanda was born until her parents divorced. So her dad's heart was never really in her home, even during the few years that he lived there.

Amanda wanted desperately to be the object of her father's love, to be the center of her daddy's attention, but even during his brief visits following the separation, Amanda felt that she ranked below the television.

> After he had moved out, my dad often came over on Sunday evenings to have dinner with us. We would set the table, put out all the food, and then pick up the table and move it into the family room so Dad could watch *60 Minutes* on TV.
>
> Dinnertime had a militant atmosphere. We couldn't put our elbows on the table, we had to pass the food to the left, and we had to eat everything on our plates. And under no circumstances could we reach for something on the table. If anyone broke these rules, they were in for an earful from Dad. He once told us about a time in Vietnam when a guy reached across Dad's plate one too many times, and he stabbed him in the hand with his fork.

Though her stomach was full after the occasional meals with her father, Amanda's heart, her love tank, consistently remained empty.

She wanted her daddy to tell her that she was beautiful. That she was special. She wanted to be held in his arms. Protected. Cherished. She wanted to be told that he loved her. That he liked her. That she was important. That she was his princess. That she mattered.

But he never did.

Same Song, Different Verse

As the years passed, Amanda experienced more of the same volatile, unhealthy home life. In her teen years, Amanda's relationship with her brother became even more strained. Erik used drugs, drank, and became verbally abusive. Amanda didn't feel safe in her own home. Fear and insecurity invaded her heart and took up residence there. Any gain of God's peace that Amanda found at church each Sunday was quickly consumed by the fears that owned her emotions at home.

A heart filled with fear is a heart filled with empty. A heart filled with any trick, scheme, or lie of Satan is an empty heart desperate to be filled. To try to fill the emptiness, some women turn to promiscuity, some to alcohol, some to work, some to excessive exercise. Amanda tried to fill her emptiness by starving herself. She became anorexic.

Living for the Moment

"I graduated from high school afraid, confused, insecure, angry, alone, and hurt," Amanda said. "Two big questions were on my mind and heart, Why this? and Why me?"

When the pages of the calendar turned to fall, Amanda packed up her belongings and traded her bedroom in for a dorm room. The car was filled to the top with Amanda's school stuff. You know, stuff like her comforter, clothes, and cosmetics—the usual college stuff. The car was also filled with her fears, insecurities, and pain.

College wasn't exactly the fresh start that Amanda needed. By the time she was settled in her dorm room, she realized that the problems she thought she left behind had followed her. The troubles that she had carefully packed in the suitcase of her heart now filled her dorm room. It was more than she could bear. She wanted to escape what she had been through. She wanted to escape the pain. She wanted to escape the empty.

Amanda's desire to fill the emptiness led her down several desperately dark paths. "I drank and partied my first two years of college with a flock of friends I shouldn't have made," Amanda said. She hung with her new friends and with a new boyfriend her whole freshman year. They were one big gang of hurting people who lived for the moment and made up their own rules. While hanging with that group, Amanda began to close out the world.

> I decided to shut myself off emotionally from others and live my life for me. Everything was, and always had been, unstable in my life. I felt insecure with who I was as a young woman. I just didn't want to let anyone get close to me. I didn't want them to be able to cause me pain. So life became all about me.

The only person Amanda dared to open up to was her boyfriend. His attention was the emotional fuel that her love tank needed that first year of college.

Starved for Love

Her sophomore year started on a horrible note, however, when the guy Amanda had been dating broke up with her. It came out of the blue, and she was stunned. After the break-up, Amanda's already-fragile world began to spin out of control. Her view of herself was jaggedly distorted. She felt completely insignificant. Her dad didn't want her. Her brother didn't like her or want her around. And now this guy, who she had given herself to sexually and who had shown such interest in her, didn't want her either. She didn't know what to do with the hurt, so she did what she could to fill the emptiness on her own.

"I didn't feel loved. Didn't feel good enough. I didn't like myself. So I tried to get rid of the pain. I tried to control what was out of control by taking diet pills and by not eating. When I did eat, I took laxatives so I could get rid of everything."

Anorexia quickly became Amanda's route of perceived escape. She thought she could eliminate her emotional pain if she was distracted by physical pain. The constant hunger caused Amanda to have a nervous stomach so that when she did eat, it was physically painful. She didn't mind the hunger. She welcomed it. The hunger somehow took the edge off her deep emotional emptiness.

Running became another obsession. Amanda ran all the time. She loved losing weight and thought she was in control of her life for the first time. On campus, she became known as "Anorexic Amanda." She found that nickname to be strangely satisfying.

Though her sophomore year was filled with empty, destructive living, she wandered into a Campus Crusade for Christ meeting a few times the second semester. But her soul was willfully shut off from God. No spiritual growth or healing came of her attendance. A war raged inside her mind, heart, and soul. The lying enemy constantly tried to get in her head and keep her heart from healing. She heard things like: "You're not worth anything. You're fat. No one's really your friend. Nobody cares about you. Who are you trying to kid? You aren't going to amount to anything. People here pretend to like you, but they really don't. What's there to like about you anyway?"

The lies and the pain kept Amanda chained to anorexia. She lived in a dorm room by herself, so she had no accountability. Her daily diet consisted of a six-pack of Mellow Yellow and few bags of Nipchee crackers. When she went home for the occasional weekend, her mom and stepdad noticed her weight loss, but thought it was a result of the pressures of college and school work.

Help on the Horizon

When Amanda moved back home for the summer after her sophomore year, her mom noticed a drastic weight change and a defiant attitude. She asked probing questions that unveiled both Amanda's eating disorder and her sexual activity. She insisted that Amanda see a doctor right away for a full physical. The doctor confirmed that Amanda had an eating disorder. That summer, Amanda's mom tried her best to get her daughter better, and Amanda began to recover. As she improved physically and waded through the clutter of her mind, the Lord began to soften Amanda's heart.

New house rules were set in place. In an effort to protect her daughter, Amanda's mom said that she had to switch colleges. Though angry and reluctant, Amanda agreed because she didn't want to rock the boat at home. Amanda's mom and stepdad were paying attention to her, and she didn't want to disappoint the only people who seemed to care. As frustrated as she was, Amanda stuffed the emotions of it all deep in her heart.

Holding those emotions down was like trying to keep a beach ball under the water. Halfway through summer, Amanda defiantly changed her mind. She wanted to go back to her university. Her parents said that she would have to pay for it by herself, but Amanda didn't care. She was determined. In only a month and a half, she had earned the money she needed for school.

The Difference

Amanda's parents told her that she could return to school only under the condition that she go to church. Amanda agreed. She began the fall semester of her junior year attending Campus Crusade meetings, but fell right back into bad habits and unhealthy thinking. The war was still raging in her mind. She wrestled with accepting condemning, empty thoughts as truth. The truth that God loved her, cherished her, chose her, and wanted to heal her still seemed too good to be true.

Amanda started dating a basketball player who was a committed Christian. It was a pure and positive dating relationship, like none she had ever had. She felt safe with this young man. He respected and encouraged her and lived life to the full. He was also the son of a local pastor, so she began to attend his father's church with him. After service one Sunday, Amanda's new beau took her aside to have a life-changing conversation that went something like this:

"I can't date you anymore," he said simply yet compassionately. "I know that you aren't the one that God has planned for me."

Amanda didn't understand. They had been seeing each other for only four weeks.

How in the world can he be dumping me already? she wondered.

He clearly felt bad and didn't intend to hurt her.

"I'll see you at church tonight, right?" he asked gently.

"No! Why would you even ask me that?" Amanda said. "Why in the world should I ever come back here?"

"Because you know the difference now," he said.

She knew exactly what he meant. And he was right. God used him in that moment to lovingly communicate truth to her heart. She knew the difference now. The difference between what the world had to offer compared to what the Lord had to offer. The difference between destruction from the enemy and healing from a loving God.

A Father's Love

That afternoon Amanda knelt on her dorm room floor and wept as truth cleared away the clutter in her mind. Love was the difference, and love is found in God for "God is love" (1 John 4:8). As she called on the Lord to change her dark life, a light went on in her heart. She recognized that God, the Spirit of truth, offered her unconditional love and forgiveness that would make her life full, and that Satan, the spirit of falsehood, offered her emptiness and death. It was all so clear:

One side was eternally bad; the other side was eternally good.

One side offered her emptiness, rejection, brokenness, and pain; the other offered her acceptance, healing, love, and hope.

One side offered lies; the other offered truth.

She knew the difference! The difference between empty and full is love—love that is found in Jesus that restores you to God the Father. Amanda, who had spent her whole life longing to be loved by her earthly daddy, now fell into the arms of her heavenly Daddy. That afternoon, she made a covenant promise with God to not ever starve herself again. Her empty was changed to full.

Her complete healing from anorexia was a gradual one. It wasn't easy. She kept her covenant with God, but sometimes she was able to eat only small amounts. Amanda got involved with church. The enemy tried to maintain the strongholds of fear, doubt, insignificance, and insecurity. "You know the difference" kept ringing in her mind. There were many days that she determined to hold on to truth even when she didn't feel it.

Wailing into Dancing

It's been twelve years since Amanda committed her life to the Lordship of Jesus Christ. She daily experiences the abundant life, the full life, because of the love of her heavenly Father. But she still struggles sometimes. Don't we all? There are still days when Amanda feels unloved and unimportant. It's the little things that can set her off. If her husband doesn't respond to her in a way that meets her needs, she might feel unloved, or when her children don't behave properly, she might feel like a failure. The old lies constantly try to pass themselves off as truth. But now Amanda *knows* truth and *knows* full life. So she presses on. She knows that she "knows the difference." The difference between wailing and dancing. Between ashes and beauty. Amanda knows the difference between empty and full.

The psalmist David says to God,

> You turned my wailing into dancing;
>   you removed my sackcloth and clothed me with joy,
> that my heart may sing to you and not be silent.
>   O LORD my God, I will give you thanks forever.
>
> (PSALM 30:11-12)

There will be times when you will wail, times when you will be desperate for a dance of love, for healing. There will be times when sackcloth and ashes keep you from joyful living. Remember that God is "the same yesterday and today and forever" (Hebrews 13:8). He was faithful to turn David's wailing into dancing and his grieving heart into a heart filled with joy. He was faithful to turn Amanda's rejection into acceptance and her empty into full. He will do the same for you. He even "knows what you need before you ask him" (Matthew 6:8).

A Deeply Troubled Woman

The Old Testament book of 1 Samuel tells the story of Hannah, one of two wives (yes, cringe with me, I said one of two wives) married to a devout Jew named Elkanah. The other wife, Peninnah, bore children, "but Hannah had none" (1 Samuel 1:2b).

From the context of chapter one, it is painfully obvious that Peninnah was not a friendly "other wife." She was gritty and difficult and downright cruel to Hannah. My girlfriend Mary Southerland would call Peninnah a sandpaper person.

Do you have a few of those in your life? If you struggle with a complex family dynamic or a seemingly impossible situation, take heart! Hannah has been there, done that, and burned the T-shirt, and she endured her challenges with admirable grace and dignity. We can learn a great deal from Hannah.

Year after year the family made a journey from their hometown of Ramathaim to Shiloh, the religious center at that time for the nation of Israel. They went for the three traditional Jewish feasts held at the tabernacle: the Passover with the Feast of Unleavened Bread, the Feast of Weeks, and the Feast of Tabernacles.

"Whenever the day came for Elkanah to sacrifice, he would give portions of the meat to his wife Peninnah and to all her sons and daughters. But to Hannah he gave a double portion because he loved her, and the LORD had closed her womb" (1 Samuel 1:4-5).

Back in those days, the culture dictated that a childless woman was pretty much a worthless woman. She was a failure. An embarrassment to her husband to the degree that he could legally divorce her just for being barren. So Hannah was a woman with some serious problems.

"And because the LORD had closed her womb, her rival kept provoking her in order to irritate her. This went on year after year. Whenever Hannah went up to the house of the LORD, her rival provoked her till she wept and would not eat" (vv. 6-7).

Hannah admitted, "I am a woman who is deeply troubled" (v. 15). Her problems weren't brief and they weren't simple. They were year-after-year problems that made her feel empty and frustrated. Her infertility was socially embarrassing, humiliating, and beyond her control. Her rival-wife problem was just as complicated. She had to live in close quarters with a difficult person. Peninnah really knew how to push Hannah's buttons, and this particular time at the tabernacle, Hannah was provoked until she broke.

Her husband tried to comfort her by saying, " 'Hannah, why are you weeping? Why don't you eat? Why are you downhearted? Don't I mean more to you than ten sons?' " (v. 8). As much as Elkanah loved Hannah, his encouragement did not bring her comfort. Nothing he could say or do could change her problem. Her soul was holding a whole lot of empty.

A Soul Poured Out

Hannah did the only thing that could possibly help her: she cried out to the Lord.

> In bitterness of soul Hannah wept much and prayed to the Lord. And she made a vow, saying, "O Lord Almighty, if you will only look upon your servant's misery and remember me, and not forget your servant but give her a son, then I will give him to the Lord for all the days of his life, and no razor will ever be used on his head (vv. 10-11).

As Hannah continued to pray, Eli the priest watched her. "Hannah was praying in her heart, and her lips were moving but her voice was not heard" (v. 13). I love that verse. She prayed with her heart, not with her mouth. Words are cheap, even in prayer if they are said carelessly, but words that are prayed *from the heart* please the Lord. Don't forget that when you pray. God looks at your heart. "The Lord does not look at the things man looks at. Man looks at the outward appearance, but the Lord looks at the heart" (1 Samuel 16:7b).

As he observed her, Eli thought that Hannah was drunk, and he rebuked her and told her to stop drinking. After all the stink Hannah had to put up with from Peninnah, now she's wrongfully accused by the priest! This poor girl couldn't catch a break. But her response was filled with God-honoring humility and vulnerability.

" 'Not so, my lord,' Hannah replied, 'I am a woman who is deeply troubled. I have not been drinking wine or beer; I was pouring out my soul to the LORD. Do not take your servant for a wicked woman; I have been praying here out of my great anguish and grief ' " (vv. 15-16).

Her answer wasn't sassy. It wasn't filled with anger at the false accusation. It was filled with truth. When we are wrongfully accused, you and I should respond with honesty and humility as Hannah did.

Hannah took her problems to God. Who do you cry to when you are deeply troubled? Do you pray with words or pray with your heart? Do you pour out your soul to the Lord or just pepper Him with vague requests? Hannah didn't just briefly bend a knee here, *she poured out her soul.* She poured out her sorrow, her disappointments, her frustrations, her depression, her confusion, her anger, her embarrassments, her anguish, and her grief.

She poured out her emptiness.

And guess what? God filled her with the fullness of His peace! He is so faithful. She was changed in the presence of the almighty Lord. But realize this: Hannah didn't just do a "drive-through" prayer time with God. She parked there for a while and did some serious business with God.

Have you done any serious business with God lately?

Are you dealing with any difficult people?

Are you faced with any seemingly impossible situations?

God looks on the heart of each woman. When you get serious with God—when you get real honest and pour out your soul to Him—He will faithfully replace your empty with the fullness of His peace, whether he removes your burdens or allows them to remain. Don't doubt it for a minute, friend. "All things are possible with God" (Mark 10:27).

Peace from God's Presence

Look what happens with Hannah next: "Eli answered, 'Go in

peace, and may the God of Israel grant you what you have asked of him'" (v. 17). He believed her and he blessed her. Hannah's pure heart must have reflected from her face as she spoke to the priest. Scripture says,

> As water reflects a face,
>   so a man's heart reflects the man.
>
> (PROVERBS 27:19)

I told you that God filled her heart with peace. Here's the evidence: "She said, 'May your servant find favor in your eyes.' Then she went her way and *ate something*, and *her face was no longer downcast*" (v. 18, emphasis mine). She ate, and her face was no longer downcast! Those are pretty clear indicators that Hannah's depression was lifted. She was filled with God's peace and His hope. But Hannah's peace did not require that the circumstances of her trial be lifted. She was not yet pregnant and she still had troubling issues. Hannah was "no longer downcast" because she experienced the one and only life-changing God in the chamber of His presence. She welcomed God's peace to the extent that she did not withhold worship in her trial.

Have you ever done that? Been mad at God and withheld your worship from Him? God can handle your anger, but be careful not to withhold your worship from Him. He is worthy in everything, whether He chooses to give or take away.

"Early the next morning they arose and worshiped before the LORD and then went back to their home at Ramah. Elkanah lay with Hannah his wife, and the LORD remembered her. So in the course of time Hannah conceived and gave birth to a son" (vv. 19-20a).

The baby's name was Samuel, and Hannah and Elkanah followed through on their commitment to give him back to God. After Samuel was weaned, they delivered him to Eli the priest to be raised in the tabernacle and brought up to serve God. Hannah gave the Lord what was most precious to her. She gave Him the very thing she had desperately prayed for. And Samuel went on to become a prophet, a priest, and the greatest judge Israel ever had.

What about you? Is there something that you're holding onto that needs to be given to the Lord? A child? A husband? A parent? A sandpaper person? With fervent worship and persistent prayer, Hannah sought God's heart, and He "remembered her." He hears your prayers too. He cares about your struggles. He cares about your relationships. He loves you and wants you to pour out your soul to Him. When you call on the name of Jesus, *all* things are possible.

Will you pour out your empty? I hope so. Once you do, He will do the rest.

He will heal your hurts and replace lies with truth.

Hang in there, friend! No matter what you are facing, call on the Lord. He will turn your empty into full.

> The LORD will guide you always;
>> he will satisfy your needs in a sun-scorched land
>> and will strengthen your frame.
> You will be like a well-watered garden,
>> like a spring whose waters never fail.
>
> (ISAIAH 58:11)

"This Life"
Words and music by Gwen Smith

My life just hasn't been the same since I met You
You've decorated my soul
Refined, retuned, renewed the passion deep inside me
Raging rivers of joy now overflow

You've got me feeling this way
The night inside me has been replaced
You've got me reaching up high
Now I'm joyful, I'm complete and I am satisfied in this life

A puzzle can't be finished if it's missing even one piece
You need them all to complete it
My spirit needed You to fill the void in my life
You just needed me to commit

No man is an island if he is set free
You came to give life more abundantly

6
Shattered Matters

But we have this treasure in jars of clay to show that this all-surpassing power is from God and not from us. We are hard pressed on every side, but not crushed; perplexed, but not in despair; persecuted, but not abandoned; struck down, but not destroyed.

2 CORINTHIANS 4:7-9

I've been through hard times. I've asked the question *why* on many occasions. I've begrudgingly said goodbye to family and friends in order to say hello to strangers and scary new places. I know the matter of being shattered.

There was a season when Brad and I lived in four different homes, in four different states, within four years. It was a very difficult time of my life. From Ohio to Pennsylvania to New York to North Carolina, we made our way across the East Coast with three little ducklings in tow. Back then, the uncertainty of what tomorrow held in store caused me a great deal of stress. A certain muscle in my back is twitching just thinking about it.

The chaos began back in 2000…

The spring and summer were crazy busy. We lived in a snuggly little town just outside Akron, Ohio, where Brad and I had settled after we got married in 1993. God had just nudged me into public music ministry. He asked me to join Him on a new faith adventure, and I said, "Yes!" So, after much praying and planning, I sifted through a list of songs I had written, connected with a producer, flew to Nashville, and recorded my first CD. Did I mention that I also had two very active little boys under the age of three and that I was pregnant with our third child? (Go ahead, laugh at me. The timing didn't make sense to me either.)

I was a stay-at-home mom. The concerts that were scheduled to follow the CD release were all within hours of our home, so we traveled as a family. God had swung open the doors of ministry opportunity, and I was delighted to step through them.

At the same time, Brad was doing really well with his company. His boss had nothing but good things to say about him and was excited to help him get promoted. It was also a time of rapid and rich spiritual growth for Brad. He became the leader of our adult Sunday school class at church and led admirably. I was so proud of him.

We loved our church, were plugged into ministries, and got along famously with our neighbors. We were comfortable and content. Very settled. Life was good.

Now, I don't know about you, but it seems to me that God doesn't necessarily always want us to be comfortable and content. (I say that tongue in cheek, of course.) Our comfort turned to chaos quickly when, just weeks before Kennedy was born, Brad accepted a job promotion that would uproot us from Akron and transplant us in Philadelphia.

A Shattered Matter

Saying goodbye to our friends, our neighbors, and our church family was torture. Brad and I had blossomed into young adults in Ohio. We exchanged our sacred marriage vows there. Gave birth to our babies there. We grew in faith as a family there.

With each farewell, the weight of sadness grew heavier. When moving day arrived and all the boxes had been loaded, we hugged our neighbors one last time, then drove away. As our home faded from sight in the rearview mirror, I realized that a part of my heart would always remain in Ohio.

Once we got to our new house, I didn't know which way was up. I cried buckets of tears out of frustration, exhaustion, and sadness.

Tension and stress became my new closest friends. The moment I said *yes* to God, so much of what had been comfortable and familiar was stripped away from my life. I don't think for one second that the timing was coincidental. God allowed what was comfortable to be removed. He then led me to a place where I would have to trust Him and lean on Him in ways I never had before.

Broken became my middle name.

I hung up my "microphoned-ministry call" when we moved to our new home. The only thing I could do was hunker down, spread out my motherly wings, and care for the babes in my nest. I changed diapers, chased toddlers, and cherished naptimes for almost a year. Friendships blossomed between me and other young moms, and the ladies' Bible study at church became a vital link to both God and other women. As I studied Scripture, the Lord began to birth new songs in my heart, and although I wasn't serving in music ministry right then, I processed my faith and life by writing songs.

Fourteen months after our move, when the chaos had finally turned to calm, Brad hesitantly announced that it was time to move again. His boss wanted him to take over a territory in Syracuse, New York. I thought perhaps we were the punch line in someone else's joke. I'm not a huge fan of snow. Brad and I always said we wanted to live in a sunny, warm place. Now we were heading farther north. Yuck. We prayed fervently about the move and felt God leading us in that direction, but I wondered if God's compass was broken. As we packed boxes once again, questions danced around in my mind.

Had I heard Him wrong?

Why in the world would God call me to a task and then herd me across the country like a nomad's cow?

Starting over in New York had a strangely familiar feel. The first few months were busy and lonely. I spent a lot of time meeting neighbors, figuring out the aisles at the new grocery stores, and finding out the best routes to take to Wal-Mart, to the post office, and to the pediatrician's office. Finding a new church was a whole nother challenge. But, in time, the matters of being shattered about the move eventually lessened as we assimilated into the community and plugged into a wonderful church family.

The Syracuse summers were lush, but the winters were long. Though snow fell often, to the tune of 150 inches a year, God's grace fell even more. He blessed me with deep friendships, intense Bible studies, and godly leadership from the pastors at our church. Brad and I immersed ourselves into the community, even though we anticipated that our time in New York would be brief. And we began to settle in.

Then, seventeen short months after we unpacked in Syracuse, a phone call from a friend in Charlotte, North Carolina, resulted in our packing for another move. Brad accepted a new, can't-pass-it-up business opportunity, and we moved to sunny North Carolina.

What an exhausting journey. With each move I experienced both bitter and sweet moments, but the aftertaste of the bitter moments seemed to linger a little longer than the sweet ones.

It was a difficult four years.

I've heard it said, "If the mountain was smooth, you couldn't climb it." There's a lot of truth to that. Through the mountain of pain I scaled in each move, God brought me closer to Him and taught me important lessons that I surely wouldn't have learned otherwise. Lessons about trusting God with my friendships, with goodbyes, with loneliness, with my family, with anger, stress, and faith. Through it all, I've come to know this for sure: in all things—even the hard things—God is sovereign and can be trusted.

He can be trusted with your family and with your finances. He can be trusted with your health and with your wealth. He can be trusted in times of victory and in times of misery. He can be trusted in your sunny celebrations and in your shattered matters.

In his article, "When Satan Hurts Christ's People," John Piper encourages us to place God in His proper place:

> When huge pain comes into your life—like divorce, or the
> loss of a precious family member, or the dream of wholeness
> shattered—it is good to have a few things settled with God

ahead of time. The reason for this is not because it makes grieving easy, but because it gives focus and boundaries for the pain.

Being confident in God does not make the pain less deep, but less broad. If some things are settled with God, there are boundaries around the field of pain. In fact, by being focused and bounded, the pain of loss may go deeper—as a river with banks runs deeper than a flood plain. But with God in his firm and proper place, the pain need not spread out into the endless spaces of ultimate meaning. This is a great blessing, though at the time it may simply feel no more tender than a brick wall. But what a precious wall it is!²

Rosetta's Story

Rosetta has run into her fair share of brick walls. She has experienced deep pain and dangerous times that have taught her to trust in the Lord with all her heart. She could've used her circumstances to justify raising her fist in anger to God, but instead, Rosetta prayerfully allowed Him to use the shattered matters of her life to draw her close to her Deliverer.

Rosetta was born and raised in a small, rustic village in Liberia with no running water, no electricity, and no roads. As a little girl, she made her own toys and played with other village children after their work in the fields was completed. School had never been an option for Rosetta. No education was available for the children of her village. Kids as young as three and four years old were expected to work on the farm to help their families survive.

Rosetta had a close family and was deeply loved by her parents. She felt safe with them. They worked hard just to live, but their home was full of love and warmth.

When she was eight years old, her older brother came back to the village from the capital city of Monrovia. He explained to his parents that Rosetta could have a chance to be educated and have great opportunities in the city. Rosetta's parents wanted her to have a good life and felt that sending her to the city with her brother was a hope-filled option.

When it was time to head to Monrovia, Rosetta's brother accompanied her in a curious, motorized travel machine. She had never seen a car before, only canoes. Filled with trepidation and wonder, she took a seat in the taxi and waved goodbye to her family and friends.

Rosetta's first challenge in the big city was overcoming the language barrier. The dominant language of Monrovia is English, and Rosetta knew only her village language of Bassa. She struggled to understand and to be understood.

Her brother had made arrangements for Rosetta to live with and work for a single woman named Mrs. Jones, a tall, slender black woman who turned out to be an abusive guardian. She had actually brought Rosetta into her home to work as a slave. For three years, Rosetta was subjected to harsh treatment, many beatings, and unsafe living.

Rosetta did what she needed to do to survive. She had come to Monrovia to get an education, but she was always at Mrs. Jones's beck and call, so she went to school only as often as Mrs. Jones would allow. Food was hard to come by. She wasn't given her own plate at dinnertime, but was told to eat the crumbs and leftovers of her guardian.

Her housing conditions were equally grim. From the age of eight to eleven, Rosetta was forced to sleep on the cold, hard ground in the unsafe hallway of Mrs. Jones's apartment building. She had no covers to keep her warm. No pillow to rest her head on. In a hallway filled with unsettling noises, Rosetta was terribly afraid every night. She didn't get a good night's sleep for three years.

By the grace of God, she was spared from bodily harm in that vulnerable environment. The emotional wounds from being separated from her parents and from living as a slave, however, were too much to take, and Rosetta fled from Mrs. Jones when she was eleven.

Over the next few years, Rosetta lived with various family members and friends in the city, attended school, and worked odd jobs. She became pregnant when she was just seventeen and gave birth to her first child, a son, at eighteen and a second child, another son, at the age of twenty. She cherished her boys and, like most mothers, determined in her heart that she would love and protect them at all times.

To make ends meet, Rosetta worked during the day and continued taking classes at night. Family and friends helped her out with the boys, and after years of hard work, Rosetta earned an associate degree in accounting.

In her late twenties, she went to work for a large company in Monrovia and was often sent to get take-out lunch orders from a local restaurant. The host of the restaurant was a Christian man from Ghana who invited Rosetta to visit his church. The Lord began to draw Rosetta to His heart once she began to attend church, but it took months for her to accept Him as Savior.

> I didn't give my heart to the Lord right away because I looked at the people and thought, *There's no way I can be like them.* I had two kids and had lived in a godless way for so long, I didn't feel worthy. The people of that church looked so holy. I felt like I had to get myself clean because God was just too holy to take me the way that I was.
>
> Once I understood that God loved me and that He died for me—that even if I had been the only one on earth, as sinful as I was, Jesus still would've died just for me—I cried and cried. My life was changed. I just wanted to go live at church! Knowing that God loved me and that He forgave me, I was a new woman.

Though her heart had been changed by the love and forgiveness of God, Rosetta had great difficulty trusting God with her children. She regularly suffered panic attacks and was gripped by fear about her boys. When she was working, Rosetta often had terrible thoughts about things that could be happening to them. God eventually freed her from these fears through desperate shattered matters.

At that time, Rosetta had an enviable position working for the American embassy in Monrovia. Then civil war broke out in December of 1990.

Early one Sunday morning Rosetta was on her way to church when the cab she was riding in was struck head-on by a pickup truck driven by a drunken soldier. Rosetta was pinned in the car and felt as if she was dying, as if her breath was leaving her body. As she waited for help to arrive, Rosetta called on God, "Lord, please don't let me die!" All she could think of was her boys. She wanted to live for them.

Fully conscious but in shock, Rosetta was cut out of the cab by a Good Samaritan with an ax. She had several serious wounds from the collision, but her primary injury was to her right foot. When she was freed from the wreckage, Rosetta's foot dangled from strips of flesh. She was immediately rushed to the hospital in Monrovia.

Due to the war, there was spotty electricity and minimal supplies at the hospital. Pain medication wasn't available either, so Rosetta lay on a gurney in excruciating torment that she describes as "the pain of having ten babies." The hospital was short staffed because many of the doctors had fled the country in the early days of the war.

On the streets, government soldiers fought against rebel troops, who moved in and plundered her neighborhood. Homes were ransacked and burned down. Money was stolen. Men, women, and children were tortured and killed. Women were raped. Danger loomed around every corner.

Rosetta suffered two days of excruciating pain and excessive heat. The bone specialist who examined her told her that she would never be able to walk or use her foot again. Rosetta clung to God more tightly than she ever had before. Every waking moment that she wasn't with family, Rosetta spent in prayer.

When Rosetta's friends from the embassy learned about her injuries, they went to the hospital and saw the primitive care she was receiving. They then returned to the embassy to pull a few strings on her behalf.

Rosetta was transferred to a missionary hospital where better medical care was available. God had heard her prayers. She had surgery on her foot, and though her stay at the hospital should've been at least one week, Rosetta had to leave just one day after her surgery in order to avoid a military raid.

When she arrived home, her neighborhood was again under attack by rebel troops. She and her sons grabbed a few essential items and left their home behind. Providentially, a friend came by with a truck and swept them out of the city just in time.

As she fled to a village, Rosetta was in severe pain. Her foot began to turn black. Her whole body was affected by the damage to her foot and her health rapidly declined. Rosetta's only hope was to have additional surgery and medical treatment. So she turned to God and cried out to Him.

God provided a way for her to get to another country for surgery, but to her great dismay, it required that she leave behind her two precious boys. What is a young mother to do when faced with either certain death or abandoning her children in the midst of a raging civil war?

She prays.

Rosetta wept to God and asked Him, "How can I leave my kids?"

For years, Rosetta's biggest fears centered around her children. Now God had allowed circumstances to invade Rosetta's life that caused her to face her fear. To live she must leave.

As Rosetta kissed her boys goodbye, she cried until she had no more tears and prayed that God would allow her to one day be reunited with her sons. Her Deliverer and Protector gently impressed on her heart that He would watch over them—and that she could trust Him. She felt Him saying, "When they are behind the house playing, I am with them. I see what they do all the time. When you are in your room sleeping and they are playing outside, I watch them 24/7. I will continue to watch over them. Trust Me."

Sometimes our biggest challenge as moms is being separated from our kids. When a mother is separated from her children, it's painful. Especially when the circumstances are beyond her control. There's such a deep bond between a mother and her child. When that bond is threatened or severed, we hurt big time. These are our children! We want to nurture, love, and protect them. I'd do anything for my kids. I'd fight the playground bully, donate a kidney, surrender all my earthly possessions, and, if necessary, I'd even die for them. I'd go to extreme measures to protect my children. You would to. It took every ounce of courage Rosetta had to let them go. When she said goodbye to her sons, she left them in the earthly care of her close friend, but ultimately, she left them in the care of her Lord.

Rosetta had no choice but to leave her boys behind. It was her only chance for survival, and therefore, the only chance that she could care for her boys in the long run. God was with her each step of the journey. Rosetta prayed fervently and leaned on His strength. Through each prayer and through His Word, God grew her trust in Him.

Rosetta made it out of Liberia safely and got the medical care she needed. Beyond that, God placed people in her path who helped her return to Liberia in the middle of the war and extract her children. Prayer after prayer was met with miracle after miracle. God was faithful in every situation.

Rosetta says, "I've learned that I should trust Him in everything. Nothing is too big or too small for God." Death was all around her, and Rosetta couldn't see how she could come out alive, let alone be healed to walk again and be reunited with her sons. But God made a way.

Would Rosetta have learned how to trust God if she hadn't had to hand her children over? I'm not sure. But she readily acknowledges that God used that painful surrender to teach her to trust and depend on Him more. She was desperate for His intervention, and she leaned into His strength when she had none of her own.

Like Rosetta, you can turn to God in your times of trouble. In what situation might you need to trust Him more?

Naomi

The Old Testament book of Ruth is rich with examples of God's faithfulness. The story of Ruth, Naomi, and Boaz took place in a time when the people of Israel had strayed far from the Lord. Yet even in those dark days, some still chose to follow God. Naomi was one such woman. How do we know? We know she was a godly woman because there was something about her faith that attracted her daughter-in-law, Ruth, to God's heart.

Like me, Naomi was a woman who had to pack up her family and belongings and leave her home, her friends, and everything familiar to relocate to a foreign place. I moved because of my husband's new job; Naomi moved due to a famine in her hometown of Bethlehem. She, her husband, Elimelech, and their two sons, Mahlon and Kilion, moved from Bethlehem to the country of Moab. But in Moab, things went from bad to worse.

> Now Elimelech, Naomi's husband, died, and she was left with her two sons. They married Moabite women, one named Orpah and the other Ruth. After they had lived there about ten years, both Mahlon and Kilion also died, and Naomi was left without her two sons and her husband (Ruth 1:3-5).

Naomi was a God-fearing woman who endured some serious shattered matters. She had left her home in a desperate situation and experienced even greater loss in the deaths of her closest loved ones. Her circumstances were undesirable and her future looked bleak.

> When she heard in Moab that the LORD had come to the aid of his people by providing food for them, Naomi and her daughters-in-law prepared to return home from there. With her two daughters-in-law she left the place where she had been living and set out on the road that would take them back to the land of Judah (vv. 6-7).

As they prepped to leave for Bethlehem, Naomi displayed lovingkindness to her daughters-in-law as she released them from any obligation to relocate with her. She encouraged them to return to their mothers' homes (v. 8) and nudged them toward new possibilities in their home country. She wanted them to have a fresh start, even though the prospects for her were grim.

There was almost nothing worse than being a widow in the ancient world. Widows were taken advantage of or ignored. They were almost always poverty stricken. God's law, therefore, provided that the nearest relative of the dead husband should care for the widow; but Naomi had no relatives in Moab, and she did not know if any of her relatives were alive in Israel.[3]

Naomi knew that she was walking into uncertain territory as she headed home to Bethlehem. She had been gone from Bethlehem for so long that she had no idea if there was any remaining family to care for her. Naomi was gracious and kind in not wanting Orpah and Ruth to endure the hardships she would probably face. What a selfless response! When shattered circumstances were all she could see, Naomi looked past her own need to the hopes, dreams, and needs of her loved ones. When you and I face complex circumstances, we have that same opportunity to bless others in spite of the pain.

Theirs was a goodbye filled with tears, hugs, and great pain.

> Then she kissed them and they wept aloud and said to her, "We will go back with you to your people."
>
> But Naomi said, "Return home, my daughters. Why would you come with me? Am I going to have any more sons, who could become your husbands? Return home, my daughters; I am too old to have another husband. Even if I thought there was still hope for me—even if I had a husband tonight and then gave birth to sons—would you wait until they grew up? Would you remain unmarried for them? No, my daughters. It is more bitter for me than for you, because the LORD's hand has gone out against me!"
>
> At this they wept again. Then Orpah kissed her mother-in-law good-bye, but Ruth clung to her (vv. 10-14).

Ruth refused to leave Naomi's side. Determined and loyal, Ruth held tightly to the woman she loved deeply. Though our natural tendency in hard times is often to try to go it alone, I've learned from Ruth, and from my own experience, that in turbulent times it's vital that we hold fast to the ones we love.

Not only did Ruth cling to Naomi, she held tight to Naomi's God, the One true God of Israel.

> "Look," said Naomi, "your sister-in-law is going back to her people and her gods. Go back with her."
>
> But Ruth replied, "Don't urge me to leave you or to turn back from you. Where you go I will go, and where you stay I will stay. Your people will be my people and your God my God. Where you die I will die, and there I will be buried. May the LORD deal with me, be it ever so severely, if anything but death separates you and me." When Naomi realized that Ruth was determined to go with her, she stopped urging her (vv. 15-18).

A Victim of Circumstance

There are times when life isn't ideal. There are times when life doesn't seem fair. As she entered Bethlehem, Naomi lamented to friends and family not to call her by her name. "Call me Mara, because the Almighty has made my life very bitter" (v. 20). Naomi didn't try to sugarcoat or hide her pain. Her circumstances were choking the life out of her, and for a time she allowed her situation to overshadow her trust in God.

Oh, how I've been there. I bet you have too. Perhaps you are there now. Be encouraged. In time, God did a work of restoration in Naomi's life that took her from bitter to better, and in time, He can do the same for you.

Though she displayed bitterness when she returned to Israel, Naomi continued to trust her Lord. Healing didn't come to her overnight. She waded through a great deal of emotional baggage and disappointment. But Scripture shows us that even in her sorrow, Naomi maintained her faith in God. She praised Him for the kindness that

Boaz showed Ruth and spoke of God's goodness even in her uncertain times (2:19-20). She praised God in the hard times, and He restored her broken heart.

God breathed hope into the souls of Naomi and Ruth through their kinsman-redeemer, Boaz. The book of Ruth goes on to tell a fascinating story of how God lovingly cared for and blessed Naomi as He used the faithful friendship and kindness of Ruth to "renew her life and sustain her" (4:15). She went back to Bethlehem as a broken, hopeless widow and was restored by the loving hand of God.

Are you dealing with a shattered matter? Are there circumstances in your life that seem broken and irreparable? Has something caused you to become bitter? Just as God did for Naomi, He wants to transform the painful pieces of your life into beautiful blessings. He has not forgotten you. He is intimately familiar with your pain. Don't turn away from Him. Continue to trust God. He will never leave your side, and He can bring restoration to your situation just as He did for Naomi and Ruth.

Like Naomi, when I experienced difficult times through the moves, I had to *choose* to trust God. Some days I chose well. Some days I didn't. My courage to trust was bolstered by playing praise music, meditating on God's goodness, reading Scripture, and praying. Those things collectively renewed my mind and strengthened my faith.

But in the darkest moments, I just hung on to faith. When all else fails, all that's required of us is that we just hang on to our faith.

Hang On!

Whatever your circumstances...no wound of life is too infected for God to heal. No problem is too difficult for God to solve. No sin is too abominable for God to forgive. No sickness is beyond *His* ability to make well. He is able. Hang on!

I don't know the shattered matters of your life, but God does. He is able to do exceedingly, abundantly beyond all you can ask or imagine (Ephesians 3:20). Hang on!

If you are ready to walk out on your husband—God loves you and is able to heal your marriage. Hang on!

If your child is wild—God loves you and is able to change your child's heart. Hang on!

If you are barraged by addiction—God loves you and wants to satisfy your every craving. Hang on!

If you are chained by financial burdens—God loves you and will supply all your needs according to His riches in Christ Jesus. Hang on!

If you are a widow who feels abandoned—God loves you and will never leave your side. Hang on!

If you are a single mother—God loves you and is the perfect Father for your fatherless children. Hang on!

If you are battling illness—God loves you, is familiar with suffering, and is able to heal you. Hang on!

If you are single and long to be cherished by a man—God loves you and sees you as perfectly beautiful in Christ. Trust His plan. Hang on!

If you feel worthless and damaged—God loves you and considers you precious and valuable. Hang on!

If you are consumed by guilt—God loves you, knows you, and paid for that sin on the cross. Release it to *His* hands. Be free!

Hang on to Jesus, friend. Hang on to Jesus. "He will yet fill your mouth with laughter and your lips with shouts of joy" (Job 8:21).

I know from personal experience that in the painful, tear-filled days, God is still good and can still be trusted. I know He is faithful. I've witnessed His strength in my weakness. I've felt His comfort in times of loss. And though we aren't always kept from experiencing shattered matters, we never have to endure them alone.

> He reached down from on high and took hold of me;
> he drew me out of deep waters.
>
> (PSALM 18:16)

Take comfort that He knows every issue on your heart and is able to shoulder your burdens. Your challenges do not fall outside the scope of God's ability to intervene. God is mysterious, He is powerful, and He is able. When you lift your eyes from your situation and fix them on your Savior, you will find peace in the pain and strength in the struggle.

> Trust in the LORD with all your heart
>   and lean not on your own understanding;
> in all your ways acknowledge him,
>   and he will make your paths straight.
>
> (PROVERBS 3:5-6)

"My Deliverer"

Words and music by Gwen Smith

When I'm down, You run to me
Give me something to believe
Now I know security
You are my Deliverer
When I call out in dismay
Mercy wipes the tears away
So I sing and praise Your name
You are my Deliverer

My heart cries out in praise to You, my Deliverer
Praises for Your faithfulness, my Deliverer
I give thanks to You, my Lord
I will sing forever more
My Redeemer, my Reward
My Deliverer

Now I know to run to You
When I can't see what to do
'Cause I know You'll pull me through
You are my Deliverer
So I celebrate Your grace
Look to see Your holy face
Lean into that warm embrace
You are my Deliverer

7

Secrets and Accusations

*"You intended to harm me, but God intended it for good to accomplish
what is now being done, the saving of many lives."*

GENESIS 50:20

It took four years of fresco painting for the Italian Renaissance
sculptor, painter, architect, and poet Michelangelo di Lodovico
Buonarroti Simoni, commonly known as Michelangelo, to finish the
ceiling of the Sistine Chapel. Most of his time painting was spent
alone, on his back, lying on scaffolding. (How painful!) The painting
on the ceiling of the Sistine Chapel is one of the most remarkable
in the history of Western art. One thing is for sure: the process that
altered a ceiling from plain to fabulous required a lot of time, great
discipline, and the hand of a master artist. The same is true for us.
The journey from broken into beautiful is a lifelong transformation
that requires both discipline and a Master Artist.

As Michelangelo was working, I'm sure that lots of people watched
in amazement. As they looked up at the beauty of his work, I bet
they said things like, "That is the most fantastic work of art I have
ever seen!" or "Extraordinary!" To which he might have said, "It's not
done!" But did the unfinished state of the project negate that parts
of the ceiling were beautiful? No! The parts that were complete were
still extravagant and breathtaking.

Maybe this is the way God and others see our lives. It's common
for people to notice the work God has done in us and comment on
the beauty. And even though compliments are nice to hear, I've been
known to resist them. (Admit it, you probably have too.) It's not so

much a humility thing as it is an "I-don't-see-myself-as-beautiful" thing. From my limited perspective, I can see only the unfinished work. But in truth, my vantage point doesn't negate the beauty of the work God has done and is doing in my life. Real beauty isn't about a finished or flawless product. It can't be. It's not possible on this side of eternity to have completed beauty. Our restoration will be complete in the presence of God when we see Him face to face.

Mosaic Majesty

A few years back, my husband, Brad, and I visited Barcelona, Spain. We had a blast! Key highlights from the trip were the food, the rich history, and the architecture. Not to mention the fun "honey-pie-time," the rest, and the relaxation.

The food was delicious. We got to taste so many new flavors and regional specialties. It was great. I became an instant fan of tapas (small, appetizer-like meals.) We ate tons of tapas, and also got to enjoy some formal world-class meals.

The local history was intriguing. We toured like crazy. We took bus tours, walking tours, and TV tours. Basically, Brad and I were vacation nerds. We struggled to communicate with cab drivers, photographed everything, and continually referred to our English-to-Spanish dictionary as we chatted with local shop owners, street venders, waiters, and residents.

Each day our senses were loaded with new sights, sounds, and sensations. The food and history impressed us, but we were captivated by the architecture. We spent time in castles, cathedrals, and common areas crafted with splendor. Intricate architectural designs are all over the city. Even mundane things like the balconies are lovely masterpieces of iron. The city is one giant art gallery between the commanding Mediterranean Sea and steep, majestic mountains.

Matthew Simpson was an American pastor in the nineteenth century. He, too, had the opportunity to visit some of the great buildings of Europe, and in the book, *Penuel: or Face to Face with God,* he describes the mosaics he saw:

The artist takes these little pieces, and polishing and arranging them, he forms them into a grand and beautiful picture. Each individual part of the picture may be a little worthless piece of glass or marble or shell; but, with each in its place, the whole constitutes a masterpiece of art. So I think it will be with humanity in the hands of the great Artist. God is picking up the little worthless pieces of stone and brass that might be trodden underfoot unnoticed, and is making of them His great masterpiece.

That moves me. It reminds me that when the broken pieces of our lives are placed in the loving hands of our extraordinary God, they can be transformed into a divine work of beauty. Oh, how it causes me to shake my head in wonder to even consider that the holy God, the Master of all creation, the Maker of all good things, the One who hung the stars and called them each by name, the One who spoke the world into existence, would even care to hold my broken pieces, let alone arrange them, polish them, and gently transform them into something whole…something beautiful. I love the way Ken Gire says it in his book, *The North Face of God:*

When suffering shatters the carefully kept vase that is our lives, God stoops to pick up the pieces. But He doesn't put them back together as a restoration project patterned after our former selves. Instead, He sifts through the rubble and selects some of the shards as raw material for another project—a mosaic that tells the story of redemption.

Through Christ, God made a way for our shame to be covered, our guilt to be forgiven, our hunger to be satisfied, and our emptiness to be filled. He wants to shatter the lies of the enemy and replace them with His truth. God knows where you have been, what you have been through, and where you are now. He knows what your "shards of raw material" are and loves you in spite of your imperfections. His tender love is far-reaching and complete.

Your past sins do not define you.

Your painful scars do not define you.

Your present sufferings do not define you.

They are just shards of brokenness that God will use to lovingly *re*fine your beauty. The restoration from broken into beautiful is neither easy nor instantaneous. It demands a yielded heart and can be quite painful, but it comes with great reward. God will need your broken pieces—your scars, shame, insecurities, disappointments, betrayals, and failures.

Do you have some of those? Are they tucked away in a safe, do-not-enter part of your heart?

You might find it hard to hand over hurts. I get that. It's hard for me too. But difficult as it may be, it's time to hand them over and let our masterful Lord create a stunning work of beauty in you. And He's going to need all of your broken pieces to complete the mosaic.

The Stranger in Her Bed

Melody is living proof of the transforming power of God. She is a vessel whose brokenness was lovingly restored to beautifully whole. Here's Melody's testimony in her own words.

I remember the very day my world began to crumble all around me. I remember the color of the room, its distinctive smells, and the haunting question that kept running through my brain, *How did I wind up here?*

You see, I was a good Christian girl. I hadn't partied in college. I hadn't dated every guy in my freshman class. I'd gone to a Christian school. I went to church and to Friday night devotionals on campus. And most importantly, I'd waited. I'd waited until I was thirty-four to marry. I'd waited till I was married to give myself to a man. I'd waited on God to make up the differences for my sacrifice, my waiting. And yet, here I was, only two and a half years after saying "I do," sitting on the cold, paper-lined table in my doctor's examination room being tested for every sexually transmitted disease on the planet.

How could this be happening to me?

It shook the foundation of everything I believed in. I was a good girl. I tried desperately to do things the "right way." We'd gone to premarital counseling with my pastor, for crying out loud! So life for me was supposed to be, well, *good!* Yet this was not good…not good at all. And if I was really honest with myself, I'd known it from day one.

There were the weird bouts of anxiety on our honeymoon, including us not sleeping in the same bed and his inability to sleep at night. There were the strange drive-by comments of regret that he had gypped me. Comments that grew darker and more sinister as he eventually described himself as a monster. There was the promise written to my mother that he would be the spiritual head of our household, and then the refusal to let either of us be engaged in spiritual activities of any kind. There was the sudden move back to his hometown, with no arrangements for jobs or a place to live. There was his unemployment the entire first year of our marriage, and his disinterest in even looking for a job. There were the blocks of time that he would be missing and unreachable, yet he had nothing to say about his whereabouts or his activities. There were the acutely uncomfortable dynamics among his family—his ex-wife who had left him to embrace the lesbian lifestyle, his detached father, over-medicated mother, promiscuous sister, and the sexually explicit behavior of his three-year-old son. There was his obsession with the Internet, and the odd login names he designated for himself. There were his increasing demands that multiple forms of birth control be used at the same time and the suggestion that I be his girlfriend instead of his wife. And as things progressed, there were sudden out-of-town trips, women's phone numbers left on our caller ID the day of his departures, missing condoms upon his return, and the graphic personal pictures of women saved on our computer.

And there was the single journal entry, left out in plain view for me to find, expressing a hope that would rise up in him every time I was late coming home from work…a hope that I had been killed in a car accident and he would finally be free.

Yes, there were many red flags, many indicators that something was very, very wrong. I was consumed with dread, but I desperately wanted to believe the best in him. I wanted to trust that God inside of him was stronger than any of the junk he might be involved in. I wanted to fight on his behalf, to wage war as a godly wife, to defeat the enemy that was wreaking havoc in our home.

A friend sent me the book *The Power of a Praying Wife* by Stormie Omartian, and so I prayed. I prayed and I prayed. The harder I prayed, the worse things got. God surrounded me with Christian friends at work, and they prayed. The harder they prayed, the worse things got. I started going to a "Loving Your Husband" women's group with a friend, and they prayed. The harder they prayed, the worse things got. My heart was confused and my faith became fragile and insecure.

Where was the great God of Elijah? Where was my Defender and my Help in times of trouble? Where was the Good that could overcome Evil? Where was the One who said He would fight for me? Two plus two was supposed to equal four, but somehow things weren't adding up.

I consulted a Christian counseling service, and they recommended I contact the ex-wife, a classmate of mine from college. When I told her why I had called, she said she'd been waiting for two and a half years to have this conversation with me. Over the next few hours, she confirmed my worst suspicions and provided the missing puzzle pieces that finally gave me an accurate picture of the person I had bound myself to.

It was not pretty. It was not polite. It was not what a good southern Christian girl dreams about. It was in no way what I had waited so long for. Deviant exhibitionism while we were still in college that resulted in administrative discipline. Addiction to pornography, sex chat rooms, and prostitution. Secret out-of-state rendezvous with strangers he had met online. A list of schools (as he served in administration) that he had been released from due to "inappropriate (sexual) behavior" with other teachers, parents, and students that had been under his supervision. Sexual abuse done to him by his father, then his molestation of his younger sister, and now, given every indication, his son. An entire secret life filled with illicit affairs, closet homosexuality, voyeurism, and lie upon lie upon lie.

My head was swimming with all of the information. I had begun to think that I was losing my mind when in actuality, I just didn't have the complete picture. Now everything I was sensing, everything I was noticing all made sense. All of those random pieces that seemed to be floating around now had a place to land. And the complete picture was horrifying.

I kicked into survivor mode. I didn't believe in divorce. I didn't believe that something like this would happen to me. I didn't believe that God would let this happen to me. I didn't believe it. I couldn't believe it. If I ignored it, wouldn't it just go away? If I just pretended that everything was fine, wouldn't it be?

So I was sitting there in the examination room trying to explain to the doctor and nurse why I needed to be tested for every STD known to man and trying not to let the utter humiliation of it all leak through the cracks of my broken heart. I knew the doctor had "gotten it" when, to my surprise, he stopped me mid-sentence and embraced me in a hug that made me feel more human than I'd felt in a long time. He told me it was all going to be all right. And for some reason, I believed him. I saw the look of my Father's eyes in that man. I heard the sound of my Father's voice in that man, telling me, "It's all going to be all right."

All right meant that I would lose my husband. *All right* meant that I would lose my stepson. *All right* meant that over the course of a few weeks, I would lose my job, my car, and my home. *All right* meant that I would lose everything—every comfort that ensured I was "doing all right," every title that helped to define me, every connection that gave my life value and purpose. I felt as though I were floating around in some weird orbit, not touching ground, no longer a participant in my life, but having been rendered invisible, detached, and completely powerless. *All right* meant that what I had waited thirty-four years for would be over in just two and a half.

From Anxiety to Appreciation

The days of waiting for the test results were excruciating. What if I had an STD that I'd have to carry the rest of my life? Or worse, what if I had AIDS? I just couldn't bear the thought. "34-year-old virgin contracts AIDS after sleeping with her only sexual partner, her husband!" For a fleeting moment I was tempted to call the *National Enquirer.* It'd fit right in there with "Bat Boy Raised by Wolves!"

But as I surrendered to the humility, an odd thing started to happen. It wasn't a disease that was growing inside of me; it was gratitude. I was thankful that I hadn't gotten pregnant while bound to this man. I was thankful that he hadn't told me he loved me since our wedding day so there was no loss of intimacy to mourn over. I was thankful that he hadn't been physically or sexually abusive, considering the debased nature of his involvements. I considered myself fortunate to have experienced only his disinterest or detached behavior in the bedroom.

In place of the devastating loss came a new awareness of all the wonderful things I *did* have. I was embraced by a loving family and friends who supported me and encouraged me…even if it was against my will at times. Friends who lived nearby would kidnap me and force me to walk in the woods and breathe some fresh air or take in a movie. Other friends sent cards, letters, and emails. I had people who didn't even know me praying for me. A friend of a friend offered a studio apartment as a haven for recovery. Anonymous notes appeared in my mailbox or were tucked in my Bible at church. Groceries would appear on my doorstep. The kids from next door would attack me in my drive-way just to give me bear hugs. And in these simple, thoughtful things, I felt the arms of God embracing me, letting me know it was *all* going to be all right. I was sheltered and loved and not forgotten. I was not invisible.

In the months and years that followed, in what I call "The Dark Years," God began to do invasive surgery on me. He didn't just want to address the horrible things that had happened, He wanted to go back and heal the things that got me there in the first place. As I did the hard work of taking an honest look at things, He was faithful to expose the lies that I had believed for so, so long. Lies of being passed over, forgotten, unlov-able, leave-able, not worth fighting for. He opened my eyes to see how He had lovingly rescued me out of the trauma and chaos that was not mine to bear. It was not the life He had for me. He snatched me out of a situation that would've consumed me and most likely would've taken my life. Even through this fiery trial, He walked right beside me. He *never* left me or forsook me. He never budged an inch.

What felt like Him deserting me when times got hard became a revela-tion of just how valiantly He had rescued me from destruction. What had seemed like Him stripping everything away turned into an overwhelming sense of His restoring power in my life. As a part of His divine restora-tion plan, five years later the following Scriptures that had spoken such life to me and that I had learned to lean on in my troubled times would be read at a New Year's wedding celebration as I married the *one true* love of my life:

My lover spoke and said to me,
   "Arise, my darling,
   my beautiful one, and come with me.
See! The winter is past;
   the rains are over and gone.
Flowers appear on the earth;
   the season of singing has come,
the cooing of doves
   is heard in our land."

   (SONG OF SONGS 2:10-12)

"Therefore I am now going to allure her;
   I will lead her into the desert
   and speak tenderly to her.
There I will give her back her vineyards,
and will make the Valley of Achor ["trouble"] a door of hope.
There she will sing as in the days of her youth,
   as in the day she came up out of Egypt.
"In that day," declares the LORD,
   "you will call me 'my husband';
   you will no longer call me 'my master.'
I will betroth you to me forever;
   I will betroth you in righteousness and justice,
   in love and compassion.
I will betroth you in faithfulness,
   and you will acknowledge the LORD."

   (HOSEA 2:14-16,19-20)

So let my testimony be this: marriage is more beautiful than I ever imagined it could be. Devastation was simply the vessel that contained God's healing oil for my life. Had I not walked with Him through the valley of trouble, I would never have gotten to see the view from the mountaintop on the other side. A view filled with hope. And in the end, what eternally will remain is this: He is faithful, He is faithful, He is faithful!

Melody

God Can Redeem Anything

God *is* faithful. He can use all circumstances for His glory. To drive this point home, let's take a brief look at the life of Joseph (Genesis 37–50). Joseph was a man of integrity who did right in the eyes of the Lord, yet he faced hardship, betrayal, and temptation. As a young man, he was less than humble a few times with his ten older brothers. Okay. Straight up, he actually came across as a puffed up little braggart. His bragging fed the jealousy of Joseph's brothers because he was clearly their father's favorite child. Now granted, Joseph threw gasoline on the fire of this jealousy when he bragged about the dreams God had given him, and may have deserved a good smack upside his head for being so insensitive, but imagine how he must have felt to be thrown into a cistern and sold into slavery by his very own brothers! It chills me to the bone. Through it all, however, "the LORD was with Joseph and he prospered" (Genesis 39:2).

He found favor in the eyes of Potiphar, an official of Pharaoh in Egypt, and gained great position, privilege, and prestige. Not so bad for a guy who had been sold into slavery, huh? God was surely with him through it all. Joseph was trusted and placed over all that Potiphar owned.

His circumstances had taken quite a turn for the better...until he was wronged again, this time by Potiphar's lying, lustful wife. Although he nobly resisted her sexual advances, Joseph was imprisoned when she falsely accused him of attempted rape. In the darkness of a dungeon, Joseph again experienced the lavish light of God's faithfulness as he was granted "favor in the eyes of the prison warden" (Genesis 39:21). He quickly rose to a position of power and responsibility amongst his prisoner peers and was trusted by the warden.

While imprisoned, Joseph met a cupbearer and a baker who had been in Pharaoh's service, and when each of these two men had a disturbing dream the same night, God allowed Joseph to interpret their dreams. Joseph told the cupbearer that in three days he would be freed from prison and restored to his position in Pharaoh's court (the interpretation wasn't quite so favorable for the baker). Joseph asked the cupbearer to remember him to Pharaoh, but on the third day, at Pharaoh's birthday feast, the cupbearer was reinstated and Joseph was forgotten. How frustrating would that be?

Two years later, while Joseph was still in the dungeon for doing the right thing, Pharaoh had two dreams that troubled him greatly. "So he sent for all the magicians and wise men of Egypt. Pharaoh told them his dreams, but no one could interpret them for him" (Genesis 41:8b). Finally, the cupbearer remembered Joseph and told Pharaoh of his ability to interpret dreams. Pharaoh sent for Joseph who, with God's enabling, interpreted the dreams, and Pharaoh rewarded Joseph by placing him in charge of his palace and his people.

After Joseph was placed in charge of the whole land of Egypt, he worked with integrity and fervor. He collected and stored all the excess food from the land in preparation for the famine that God had revealed, through Pharaoh's dream, would come. There were seven years of abundance followed by seven years of famine. The years of famine were severe, and during the famine, Joseph sold grain to both the Egyptians and to people of other lands.

Ultimately, the famine brought Joseph's brothers and father from the land of Canaan to Egypt for a God-reunion and restoration that only our amazing El-Shaddai could have arranged. In spite of all the pain he endured at the hands of others, Joseph was able to exclaim to his brothers in kindness, "You intended to harm me, but God intended it for good."

Joseph really got it. He saw the big picture.

Though we've had to rush through this story, the take-away is clear. Joseph paid a high price for sins that had been committed against him, but through the trials, he was blessed richly as God eventually used each circumstance for good. My dear sister, our God is able to redeem anything and everything that we face or endure. Anything! No matter what you've been through, no matter the secrets you've been hiding or accusations you've been listening to, God is able to redeem you.

Do you believe that? He is waiting to show you the big picture. If you've been holding something back from God or resisting His healing, then it's time you take your faith and trust to another level. No more safe living. Spend a few minutes in prayer right now and ask God to show you what to do next.

> And we know that in all things God works for the good of those who love him, who have been called according to his purpose (Romans 8:28).

"More Beautiful"

Lyrics and music by Gwen Smith

I hit the wall today
Felt defeated so many ways
Burned by these tears of pain
I can feel the flames from this constant strain driving me insane
Are you listening?
Can you feel this sting?
My heart is blistering

Oh, if this is where I need to be
Then every time I burn, my Lord help me to see
That I need You every hour
Your fire has the power to make me what You want me to be
More beautiful
More beautiful
Beauty from the ashes
Let me be more beautiful to Thee

I'm often drawn to You
When I'm seared by adversity
Where is my dignity?
My maturity?
Can You only see inconsistency?
Can I really shine and be purified so You'll be glorified?

[Chorus]

I don't need to understand all the ways You move Your hand
But this smoke in my eyes is making me cry
Lord, make me beautiful to Thee

8
Measuring Up

This righteousness from God comes through faith in Jesus Christ to all who believe. There is no difference, for all have sinned and fall short of the glory of God, and are justified freely by his grace through the redemption that came by Jesus Christ.

ROMANS 3:22-24

From the time I was a young girl I wanted to be beautiful. I also wanted to be loved. I wanted to be special. I wanted to be accepted. I wanted to have friends. I wanted to be a great athlete. (Trust me, this list could go on.) But *mostly* I wanted to be beautiful.

In the fifth grade, I resorted to desperate measures in a very "eleven-year-old, clueless-adolescent" kind of way. I distinctly remember some bright blue eye shadow being involved. I can even picture in my mind what that unauthorized makeup looked like in its case, like the kind that would normally hold watercolor paint. Five fabulous (or not so fabulous) color options ranging from pale green to bright blue were available to this preadolescent. Mercy!

Please keep in mind we *are* talking about the early eighties here. Blue eye shadow was all the rage. It was everywhere! On magazine covers, commercials, and on every older woman in church. I think even Marsha Brady was wearing it on TV. Trust me when I say that, back then, most of the girls my age took beauty cues from Marsha Brady. I know...scary.

I rode the bus to elementary school, which gave me a brief, unsupervised window of opportunity to misbehave and sneak around between exiting the big yellow taxi and entering the classroom. My neighbors Brenda and Sally sometimes chose to adventure with me to the West Hempfield Elementary School beauty salon: the girl's bathroom. As long as we made it to our classrooms before the bell rang, we were golden.

Enter the blue eye shadow.

I'm not sure where my eye shadow kit came from. It could've been a hand-me-down from an aunt or a family friend. It could have been a garage sale find. I don't remember. I'm certain, however, that at that point in my life, eye shadow was supposed to be for play, not for school. Not being one to get tripped up over details, I generously smudged the bright blue cream on my eyelids. Then, feeling I had reached a higher level of beauty, I proceeded to Miss Lewis's boring fifth grade class.

As I remember it, several days of eye-colored bliss passed. In my mind, I was cool and hip. In reality, not so much. During some quiet work time one morning, Miss Lewis called me up to her desk. With a hushed teacher-tone, she asked me, "Does your mother know you're wearing that eye shadow to school?"

"Yes, Miss Lewis," I said. "My mom lets me wear this."

"Well, Gwen, I might just need to call your mother and ask her about that." Then she sent me back to my seat.

I sat in fear as I entertained dreadful thoughts of being found out. Miss Lewis never did call my mom, but the day I was called up to her desk was the *last* day I wore bright blue eye shadow at school. (At least in the fifth grade.)

The truth of the matter is I just wanted to feel beautiful. I thought that if I were beautiful, people would like me better. They would accept me more. My parents couldn't afford the cool Gloria Vanderbilt jeans that were a big fashion yes, and I wanted to be liked by my friends. I cared about what other people thought about me. I wanted to measure up. To some degree, I still do.

Can you relate?

Not necessarily to the eye shadow story, but to the desire to be beautiful and to be seen as beautiful? I believe that desire is woven into the very fabric of our hearts as women.

We all want to be beautiful. And that's okay! It's fine to want to be beautiful. To take care of yourself. To gloss your lips and girdle your hips. But what we need to be cautious of is blurring the lines between physical beauty, spiritual beauty, and personal worth. Measuring up to Hollywood's version of beautiful has never been, nor ever will be, what God desires for us. God cares much more about our internal beauty, our reverence and love for Him, than our external beauty. The Bible says,

> Charm is deceptive, and beauty is fleeting;
>> but a woman who fears the LORD is to be praised.
>
> (PROVERBS 31:30)

Beauty Is Subjective

Okay, straight up: I confess that I don't have this "measuring up" battle conquered yet. I suspect that you don't either. We are bombarded by falsified standards of perfection for women on every magazine rack, on TV, in romance novels, in movies, and—dare I say—in many churches.

Measuring up.

This one's a toughie!

I promise to blend as much humor as I can into this chapter to keep us both from breaking down in tears of frustration. There's a line in the song "Broken into Beautiful" that says: "We live with accusations, sometimes heavy expectations that tell us we can never measure up."[4] The paradox of that statement is that we can measure up and we can't.

Beauty is subjective. Its standards vary from culture to culture. In his book, *Fan the Flame,* former Moody Bible Institute president Joseph Stowell convincingly illustrates this:

> I was in West Africa—Timbuktu to be exact—and the missionaries were telling me that in that culture the larger the

women were the more beautiful they were thought to be. In fact, a young missionary who had a small, trim wife said that the nationals had told him she was a bad reflection on him—he obviously was not providing well enough for her. A proverb in that part of Africa says that if your wife is on a camel and the camel cannot stand up, your wife is truly beautiful.[5]

Now that's just plain funny!

Never Good Enough

My girlfriend Denise is a knockout. She's got the whole beauty package going on. She's tall, slender, athletic, bright, and funny. To know her is to love her. But she is *so* pretty that if you didn't know her, you might love to hate her. Kind of like the supermodels.

Denise is a former model and gymnast who lived much of her life in the shadow of perfection's impossible measuring stick. She grew up in a small town just outside of Cleveland, Ohio, and made a decision for Christ as a child. Though she was a believer, Denise says she still struggled with common issues of measuring up.

> It was very important to me to be well-liked and to be successful in every aspect of my life. My family strived to be the ideal, all-American family. I worked hard to have great grades, be a great athlete, and wear the right clothes. Basically overachieve. As a model and gymnast, body type and strength were very important to winning, as well as to my identity.

By nature, Denise is competitive. Most would refer to her personality as type-A. A go-getter. A perfectionist. She's the kind of girl you want on your team: determined, focused, and disciplined. Her quest to be the best, however, left Denise feeling helpless and unsuccessful. Even though she was a fierce competitor as a gymnast, she never thought she was good enough. For years Denise tried to control the circumstances and the people in her life in an attempt to make things perfect. Eventually, her pursuit of perfection got Denise into a heap of trouble. As time-management guru Edwin Bliss has said, "The pursuit of excellence is gratifying and healthy. The pursuit of perfection is frustrating, neurotic, and a terrible waste of time."[6]

As a high school gymnast, Denise dealt with the pressures to measure up in a destructive way. She became bulimic. She wanted to be in control of her body and manage her weight, but became enslaved to an addictive and damaging behavior. She was a Christian girl who knew that God loved her. She had been told that she was beautiful to Him. But for a season of her life, Denise didn't consider that to be enough.

At first, to her delight, Denise's bulimia resulted in weight loss. Keeping extra weight off allowed her to be competitive in the gym and to look good. She wasn't alone. Most of her teammates had eating disorders too.

"What I thought was just a phase became my way of life," Denise remembers.

Her destructive behavior followed her to college. Denise thought she was in control of the bulimia, but eventually realized that bulimia was in control of her. It consumed her thoughts. It swung the gates of deception wide open for the enemy to stroll right through. He laughed all the way because he had her right where he wanted her.

Negative self-talk filled her head. A thought as simple as, *I'm a little bit nervous about teaching this fitness class,* would snowball into, *You are so fat. You should never have eaten all that food this afternoon. You're such an idiot! You won't even be able to get through this class.* The voice in her head constantly told her she didn't measure up.

"If I heard ninety-nine positive comments about myself and one negative comment, I couldn't let the one negative comment go," she said. "I illuminated my failures and shortcomings instead of celebrating my successes."

During that time, she constantly talked about her body...about how awful it was. Denise says it was as if a ticker tape was filling her mind with a steady stream of negative thoughts and beating her down.

She prayed, "Lord, help me find a way to cut that ticker tape. I need a reprieve." God eventually did cut it with truth, but it took a while for Denise to learn to recognize Satan's lies for what they were.

The Lord placed many Christian friends in Denise's path who encouraged her to see a counselor. She went, though she still wanted her way more than God's way. The counselor told her that she must *want* to be healed of her eating disorder. She needed motivation to change. Denise lacked the motivation until she went home for fall break and finally hit rock bottom.

A Time for Change

Denise was consumed with being fit. Each day of break was another opportunity to strive for physical perfection, and she trained hard. She had been fasting for a few days—something she relished because of the dramatic physical results, not for the spiritual benefits the Bible speaks of—and then ate something. The ticker in her mind told her that she should feel terrible about eating, so Denise went upstairs and made herself throw up. Her body had grown so weak that she fell to the floor before making it to her bed.

Her brother found her on the floor crying and completely out of it.

Denise's brother, who suffers from a mild form of cerebral palsy and has struggled to overcome the challenges of his disability, was alarmed and angry. Once Denise was able to get up from the floor, her brother confronted her with strong words that were the catalyst for the change she needed.

"I have worked all my life to overcome my physical deformity," he said. "And here you are intentionally destroying yourself."

In that moment, Denise felt the weight of truth and finally crumbled. Her previous casual attempts to allow God to intervene were now replaced with sincere cries for help. She needed to change and she needed God's help for the change to happen. She needed Him to consume her thoughts and transform her mind. She needed Him desperately.

Denise had known the truth from the beginning. She just resisted it. She knew that bulimia was destructive, but the pressures of the world had a greater hold on her. When she turned to Jesus for help, He began to transform her from the inside out. As a child, Denise gave her heart to Jesus. As an adult, she surrendered her life to Him. There's a big difference. In the surrendering, Denise found healing for the bulimia and emotional freedom from the need to measure up to the world's standard of perfection.

Her healing took time. It progressed slowly. God used His Word, Christian counseling, and friends to replace lies with His truth. Denise has experienced full healing through the strength of the Lord and now regularly shares her story with women and young girls.

Healing begins when we hold tightly to the truth of God and allow the truth of God to hold tightly to us. God gives each of us the freedom to accept or reject His way. When we lean into His truth, we are less likely to conform to the world. His truth, His Word can be the light for each step we take. It illuminates the path that leads to His heart. God's Word transforms. The apostle Paul said, "Do not conform any longer to the pattern of this world, but be transformed by the renewing of your mind" (Romans 12:2a).

We live in a competitive world. The pressures to be thin, beautiful, fit, smart, sexy, funny, rich, and popular trap us in a relentless vise-grip. Denise's story isn't much different from yours or mine. You don't need to be a model or a gymnast to get trapped in a disorder or an addictive lifestyle. You could be a college student, a businesswoman, a nurse, a mom, a dance instructor, a retail clerk, or a Sunday school teacher. No one is exempt. Feelings of inadequacy and inferiority ravage hearts of Christians and non-Christians alike.

Our attempts to measure up are all-consuming traps. They focus our attention inward versus upward, just as they did with Denise. When we get caught in the trap of striving to measure up, we focus on ourselves. That was never God's plan. We were designed to focus on Him. Shifting our attention from ourselves to God will change our perspective. God longs for our obsession to be Him.

"I am the LORD; that is my name!
I will not give my glory to another
or my praise to idols."

(ISAIAH 42:8)

The Dangers of Comparing

A common way we attempt to measure up is through comparison. Comparing is one of the most dangerous and destructive behaviors that we women engage in. We compare everything—our husbands, our children, our churches, and our cars. We compare our homes, our schedules, our finances, our blessings, and our burdens. There is a subtle, internal monologue that plagues our minds and causes us to pull out our measuring sticks and hold them up to the people around us.

That's not to say that we should isolate ourselves or withdraw from awareness of others. We need to be able to relate to our friends, families, and neighbors. No question. But we shouldn't compare ourselves to them.

Comparing your life, your family, your stuff, your failures, and your accomplishments to that of someone else is dangerous. Very dangerous. It draws the focus of your heart to you instead of to God. The comparing game also brews a bitter cup of jealousy and resentment. I should know. I've tasted more than my fair share of that bitter drink.

No, we in the church are not immune to comparisons by a long stretch. How many times have you looked across the aisle and thought, *She's such a godly woman. I wish I was more like her,* or *I wish I could pray like her (or sing like her, or speak like her, or bake like her, or be popular like her, or be organized like her)?*

Often the things we compare are completely meaningless, fluffy things.

Do you have a girlfriend with perfect hair? How about a girlfriend with a husband who treats her as a precious jewel? Got a friend whose house is crazy-organized? Do you have a friend who works out faithfully and looks like she belongs on the cover of a fitness magazine? Got one of those?

Sure you do.

So do I. Over the years, I've struggled with feeling inadequate. And though God has grown me in this area, I still wrestle with it sometimes. Seriously. Here are a few personal examples:

- *I don't keep a perfect home.* I've got friends who keep a perfect home: counters always wiped to shiny, floors always vacuumed, toys organized in coordinating bins, bedsheets changed weekly, and home-baked cookies in the oven 24/7. Me? Not even close. I married Mr. Neat, but I struggle to keep things picked up on my side of the closet. Baskets of clean clothes line the floor of my bedroom because I don't take the time to put them away when they come out of the dryer. When I look at the baskets, I feel like a bad wife and mother, as though I just don't measure up.

- *I don't work out as much as I should.* I've got friends with fabulously fit bodies. They go to the health club, wear cute workout outfits, and drink expensive flavored water. When they walk, their behinds don't jiggle and their arms don't flap in the wind. At one time I was a college athlete. Now I fail regularly to fit a power walk into my schedule. Seems crazy. Makes me crazy! Makes me flabby. I know I should work out more. I don't feel like I measure up to a high fitness standard.

I regret to say that my list of shortcomings could go on and on. I'm keenly aware that I fall short in many areas. It's easy to listen to the voices in your head that say, *You're not this, and you're not that. You don't do this well, and you can't do that.* Your internal comparisons form a vicious measuring stick that the enemy loves to wave in your face. Your defense in such an attack should be God's truth. You were made to be you, and are called to be uniquely you, for Him.

Yes, we should strive to live lives of excellence. And yes, we should be aware of areas that need improvement. But God intends that we should bloom where we are planted and thrive in our giftings so that His church can function in a healthy way.

In the New Testament book of 1 Corinthians, the apostle Paul shows us clearly that each of us has a divine design and an important role to play in the Body of Christ.

> For the body is not one member, but many. If the foot says, "Because I am not a hand, I am not a part of the body," it is not for this reason any the less a part of the body. And if the ear says, "Because I am not an eye, I am not a part of the body," it is not for this reason any the less a part of the body. If the whole body were an eye, where would the hearing be? If the whole were hearing, where would the sense of smell be? But now God has placed the members, each one of them, in the body, just as He desired. If they were all one member, where would the body be? But now there are many members, but one body (1 Corinthians 12:14-20, NASB).

God has a special plan for your life. God's gifts for you are the best gifts for you to possess. He fashioned you in His image and tenderly knit you in your mother's womb. You are purposed to be a God-loving you.

It's time we quit chasing the interests of others and start pursuing the passions that were written on our hearts. Our role in the Body of Christ is essential. God wants us to stop trying to measure up to everybody around us and be content in Him.

I Need a Makeover!

Have you ever wondered why we compare ourselves to others? I believe it's because we're sinful. We compare because we always fall short of God's standard and are racked with guilt. Many times I feel as though I'm just never going to get there...to that place where I don't fall short. In reality, I won't. Not until I see my Lord face to face. Every time I read my Bible I'm reminded that I need an extreme makeover. It's so hard!

The American evangelist D.L. Moody said, "The Bible will keep you from sin, or sin will keep you from the Bible."

Every one of us is aware that we fall short, yet we seem to be strangely convinced that we are the only ones sitting in the pews struggling. That's just not true. We are all bombarded with accusations from Satan. He's the accuser of the brethren. He takes great delight in taunting us and telling us that we don't measure up. When he does, don't forget that you can boldly deflect his nasty lies with God's truth. "You, dear children, are from God and have overcome them, because the one who is in you is greater than the one who is in the world" (1 John 4:4).

The Measuring Stick Has Been Removed

Measuring up isn't about what we can do or how we look. It's not about being physically strong, wealthy, or attractive. It's not about being smart enough, witty enough, thin enough, neat enough, helpful enough, or religious enough. It's about perfection...and our lack of it.

Every one of us suffers from a spiritual standard of perfection that's impossible to attain. None of us measures up to the perfect standard of a holy God. We are saved by grace, not our perfection. "For it is by grace you have been saved, through faith—and this not from yourselves, it is the gift of God—not by works, so that no one can boast" (Ephesians 2:8-9).

Jesus removed the measuring stick, sees us as perfectly beautiful, and invites us to His banquet table.

> Because of the sacrifice of the Messiah, his blood poured out on the altar of the Cross, we're a free people—free of penalties and punishments chalked up by all our misdeeds. And not just barely free, either. Abundantly free! He thought of everything, provided for everything we could possibly need,

letting us in on the plans he took such delight in making. He set it all out before us in Christ, a long-range plan in which everything would be brought together and summed up in him, everything in deepest heaven, everything on planet earth (Ephesians 1:7-10, MSG).

God loves you. His mercy reaches past your inadequacies, your inferiorities, your imperfections, and your weaknesses to the shed blood of God's perfect son, Jesus Christ, our Lord and Savior. Jesus came to earth to *remove* the measuring stick once and for all.

Grace! Grace! Grace!

God's grace isn't bound by limits, and it isn't withheld from any heart that seeks Him sincerely. "But sin didn't, and doesn't, have a chance in competition with the aggressive forgiveness we call grace. When it's sin versus grace, grace wins hands down" (Romans 5:20, MSG). God extends grace to his children because He loves us. His love is deeper, wider, and higher than we can ever imagine. Like the Energizer Bunny, God's grace keeps going and going and going. Eternally.

Grace truly *is* amazing!

The amazing grace of the Master, Jesus Christ, the extravagant love of God, the intimate friendship of the Holy Spirit, be with all of you (2 Corinthians 13:14, MSG).

"Nothing without You"

Words by Gwen Smith
Music by Gwen Smith and Robert Cowherd

In the bigness of life I'm practically invisible
In the smallness of my life, I'm big
In the length of eternity, I barely make the ruler
Yet as I live Your light can shine in me

My soul's but a mist in a torrential downpour
A vapor that fades away
My significance is nothing without you
Nothing without you

I can boast in nothing, nothing that I do
'Cause what I do is nothing, nothing without You
Yet I glory in all that You've done
You created me, You chose me, You use me

[Chorus]

In the finite days of me
Lord, it's You they need to see
As I walk this road before me
I want to take Your path
Take Your path
Take the lead

9

Valued and Adored

"The LORD your God is with you, he is mighty to save.
He will take great delight in you, he will quiet you with his love,
he will rejoice over you with singing."

ZEPHANIAH 3:17

I spin plates.

Not real plates. Metaphorical plates. I spin lots of plates at the same time. I multitask, whether it's with small household chores or with big projects. Doesn't matter. This has been both a blessing and a curse in my life. Sometimes my attention is divided in too many directions, while other times I feel invigorated, energized, and blessed by the amount of things I can get done in a small window of time.

Being a plate-spinning mom can be a real challenge at times. Okay...all the time.

When my kids want me, they don't like to wait for me to spin three more plates before I answer them. When they were smaller, they figured out a way to stop me mid-task, no matter what I was doing. They would place their chubby little hands on my cheeks, look me in the eye, and demand my full attention. Then they would deliver their message or question to their captive audience.

God wants you to pause the plate spinning and be His captive audience in this very moment. He wants you to be still, gaze into His eyes, and hear about the love He has for you. Maybe you've known of His love for years. Maybe God's love is all new to you. Regardless, it's time to stop and smell the sweet Rose of Sharon. It's time to stop for love.

I'd like you to imagine His strong yet gentle hands reaching for your cheeks, lifting your chin, and drawing your eyes to His. He wants you to fix your gaze on His blazing, mercy-filled eyes. He wants your full attention.

It's All About Love

Before God spoke the heavens and earth into existence
> before His voice lit the sun, causing darkness to separate
> from light
>> before He decorated the sky with stars and called them
>> each by name
>>> before He commanded the waters to divide from land
>>> and established living creatures to inhabit the earth
>>>> before He breathed the first breath of life over the
>>>> dust of the ground and into the lungs of Adam,
the mysterious and mighty God of the universe loved you.
Try to fathom that for a few minutes.

The mystery of God's love cannot be solved. The magnitude of God's love cannot be grasped. The measure of God's love cannot be comprehended. He loves you perfectly and eternally.

> But from everlasting to everlasting
>> the LORD's love is with those who fear him.
>
> (PSALM 103:17A)

His love is unavoidable for His children. If you are His through the blood of Jesus Christ, nothing can separate you from the love of God! The apostle Paul spoke emphatically about this to the believers in Rome:

> I am convinced that nothing can ever separate us from God's love. Neither death nor life, neither angels nor demons, neither our fears for today nor our worries about tomorrow—not even the powers of hell can separate us from God's love. No power in the sky above or in the earth below—indeed, nothing in all creation will ever be able to separate us from the

love of God that is revealed in Christ Jesus our Lord (Romans 8:38-39, NLT).

God loves you. God knows you. God wants you. God chose you. How in the world can that be true? It's a mystery. God said through the prophet Isaiah,

> "For my thoughts are not your thoughts,
>   neither are your ways my ways,"
>   declares the LORD.
> "As the heavens are higher than the earth,
>   so are my ways higher than your ways
>   and my thoughts than your thoughts."
>
>   (ISAIAH 55:8-9)

I don't even pretend to understand it. I just accept it.

God is truth. His Word is truth. His Word says He loves you and He loves me. We need to take Him at His word and trust Him at His heart. That's faith, my friend. "Now faith is being sure of what we hope for and certain of what we do not see" (Hebrews 11:1). In order to believe that God, whom we've never seen, loves us, faith is essential. Takes us right back to the basics, doesn't it?

> Jesus loves me! This I know,
> For the Bible tells me so;
> Little ones to Him belong,
> They are weak but He is strong.
> Yes, Jesus loves me!
> Yes, Jesus loves me!
> Yes, Jesus loves me!
> The Bible tells me so.

That song tells a simple truth. God loves you...because He said so. Believe it. Accept it. His love can't be earned. His love can't be bought. It can only be accepted or rejected. It's a choice. Do you accept His love?

Nailing Lies to the Cross

One major blessing of being in women's ministry is the friendships I have with other women in ministry. We are our own little band of sisters. Sisters with a mission! We cheer for one another, cry with one another, laugh with one another, pray for one another, and rejoice with one another.

One sister I've had the opportunity to lock arms with for the journey is Renee Swope. Renee works for an international women's ministry and is a talented, God-fearing, Bible-teaching speaker and writer. A few years back, Renee traveled across the country to speak at a women's retreat. When she got there, a few unexpected circumstances caused her to send out an "SOS, pray-for-me-now" email to her ministry sisters. I got the email and hit my knees.

Early the next week, Renee sent us an email thanking us for praying and telling us what God did in the hearts of women at that retreat. (Her email contained a brief story that inspired the lyrics of the song I cowrote that bears the same title as this book.) She told us that she spoke about the lies that we believe as women and told personal and biblical stories that illuminated God's truth. Then, at the final session, Renee asked the women to consider what they believed to be true about themselves. Her challenge went something like this: "When you settle your soul long enough to simply be still—when you pause to listen to your heart—what do you hear? Are there lies that linger in your heart knowingly or unknowingly?"

She encouraged them to write on a note card the lies they had accepted as truth, whether lies spoken by a parent, kids in the schoolyard, a friend, a family member, a spouse, a child, a pastor, or a stranger. She told them that some of the lies might never have been spoken at all, just believed.

When they finished she invited them to bring the cards to a wooden cross at the front of the room. Next to the cross she had placed baskets filled with promises from God's Word, and after each woman nailed her card to the cross, she picked up a *truth* that would replace her lies.

Tears ran down almost every cheek as the women brought their lies to the cross and embraced, some for the very first time, God's life-changing Words. Guilt was forgiven, worthless became precious, and sorrows were traded for joy that day. Then a whoop-it-up celebration went down! God, through his Holy Spirit, revealed His heart to those sweet women and shattered the lies of the enemy.

After the retreat was over, Renee looked through the cards nailed to the cross. One card jumped out at her. Written over and over was one word: *Worthless!*

The woman who wrote that wasn't the only one at that retreat who felt that way. That same word—*worthless*—was penned on many of the cards that weekend. It represents a lie that has been believed by most every woman at some point in her life. There have been days, weeks, and months that I've believed it myself.

It's one of Satan's favorite words to throw at us, and it is a big, fat, ugly lie.

What does your heart hear when you are still?

What lies would you write on that card?

The Bible clearly shows us that we are valued in the sight of the Lord. When we allow God's Word to flood our lives with the truth, we are changed by the height, the depth, and the width of His love for us. "Take in with all Christians the extravagant dimensions of Christ's love. Reach out and experience the breadth! Test its length! Plumb the depths! Rise to the heights! Live full lives, full in the fullness of God" (Ephesians 3:18-19, MSG).

God loves you with a personal love. He knows your name. He knit you together in your mother's womb. He considers you highly valuable. No matter what you've believed in the past, choose by faith to believe this now: You are valued, priceless, and adored by God.

The Great Adventure

God doesn't just call us to receive His love. He also wants us to respond to it. To experience it. To be transformed and restored by it.

Have you ever read that children's book, *Going on a Bear Hunt?* When my kids were little we wore out the board book we owned. It's about a family who goes on an adventure together and faces obstacle after obstacle. Each time they face a new challenge, they determine that they "Can't go over it. Can't go under it. Oh no! We've got to go through it!"

The great adventure of life is our pilgrimage to God's heart. When you place your faith in Christ, you become a child of the Heavenly Father who will never leave your side. He loves you with a stubborn love. In every case, without exception, you cannot escape or be separated from His love. You can ignore it, doubt it, and question it. But you can't be separated from it. Not if you are His.

When the psalmist experienced trouble at the hand of others, he said,

> When I said, "My foot is slipping,"
>   your love, O LORD, supported me.
> When anxiety was great within me,
>   your consolation brought joy to my soul.
>
> (PSALM 94:18-19)

Has your foot slipped lately? Are you anxious or fearful about anything? The psalmist found strength and support and joy in God's love. When we lay down our fears and anxieties before the Lord, His perfect love drives the fear away and breathes joy into our souls.

The Trumpet Game

My worship pastor has a little girl named Elizabeth. When Elizabeth was one year old, Brad and his wife taught her sign language. For the word *please,* they chose to have her rub her chest. So, as Brad and Jamie taught Elizabeth to say please, they rubbed their own chests and said "please." Simple enough.

Elizabeth had a favorite toy, a plastic knobby toy that held colorful rings. You know the one with the yellow pole and white base that, without the rings, loosely resembles a trumpet? (C'mon, use your imagination!) So, being the fun, creative parents that Brad and Jamie are, they would dump off the rings and playfully hold up Elizabeth's toy and make a trumpet sound. Elizabeth loved her parents' silliness.

She laughed and clapped with delight. It became a favorite game in their household.

One day, when Brad and Elizabeth were playing the trumpet game, Elizabeth excitedly grabbed the toy and handed it back to Brad to *do it again*. Brad encouraged her to say "please" and rubbed his chest. To his surprise, Elizabeth came over to him and started to rub *his* chest instead of her own.

Did this please her daddy? You bet it did!

Even though Elizabeth mixed up the signals, she communicated with her daddy. Brad was filled with love and joy by her effort. He was pleased that she came to him. Not because she did or didn't do something right, but just because she is his daughter and he loves her. He adores her.

God adores you too. Just because you are His child. His sweet daughter. "How great is the love the Father has lavished on us, that we should be called children of God! And that is what we are!" (1 John 3:1a).

Have you considered that perhaps God *isn't* longing for you to come to Him with perfect, polished prayers composed of fifty-cent words and flowery language? Have you thought about the pleasure God experiences when you simply approach Him just as you are, warts and all, because He loves you? He delights in your attention. He takes pleasure when you go to Him simply because you are His. I love how the psalmist responded to God's love:

> Praise the LORD, O my soul;
>> all my inmost being, praise his holy name.
> Praise the LORD, O my soul,
>> and forget not all his benefits—
> who forgives all your sins
>> and heals all your diseases,
> who redeems your life from the pit
>> and crowns you with love and compassion,
> who satisfies your desires with good things
>> so that your youth is renewed like the eagle's.
>
> (PSALM 103:1-5)

Live Love Louder

My car is a taxi. If I had a meter on the dash that demanded payment for each mom-mile traveled, I would be a rich woman. My kids and I spend a lot of time going about our business together. Whether it's a jaunt to school, a trip to the market, or a journey to one of the ten thousand ball fields in town, the activities that are penned on my calendar require much car travel.

Once we are strapped and settled, my kids inevitably ask to hear music. Now, I'm a total music chick, so you *know* I crank up the volume and jam with my kids! As the decibels rise, the music becomes a focal point of our journey. We love to listen loudly.

What song are you singing on your life journey? Is God in the chorus? Is He in the melody?

When asked about the most important commandment, Jesus responded: "Love the Lord your God with all your heart and with all your soul and with all your mind" (Matthew 22:37).

Seems simple, right? Not so fast. God's Word calls each of us to love Him with *all* of our hearts, souls, and minds. How are you doing with that? He doesn't want just a little bit of love from you, He wants the full measure. He wants first, second, and third place in your heart, soul, and mind. He wants you to turn up the volume on your love for Him. He's calling you to live love louder.

1. Love God More! God wants you to love Him *more.* More tomorrow than today. More today than yesterday. More this year than last year. He wants you to love Him when the road of life is smooth and steady. He wants you to love Him when the road is rocky and difficult. Why? Because God loved you first.

A certain medieval monk announced he would be preaching the next Sunday evening on "The Love of God." As the shadows fell and the light faded from the cathedral windows, the congregation gathered. In the darkness, the monk lit a candle and carried it to the crucifix. First, he illuminated the crown of thorns; next, the two wounded hands; then the spear wound; and finally the feet. In the hush that fell, he blew out the candle and left the chancel. There was nothing else to say.

God loves us perfectly. The greatest call in our lives is to love God in return. Our life song should be a love song. Many of us sing that tune regularly, but let's choose this day to turn up the volume on our love for God. Let's live love louder.

Take a moment to center your heart, soul, and mind on Christ right now. Worship Him in spirit and in truth. Adore Him. Praise Him. Pray that He will help you live love louder today. Sing or contemplate the lyrics of this hymn as part of your response:

"My Jesus, I Love Thee"

My Jesus, I love Thee, I know Thou art mine;
For Thee all the follies of sin I resign.
My gracious Redeemer, my Savior art Thou;
If ever I loved Thee, my Jesus, 'tis now

I love Thee because Thou hast first loved me,
And purchased my pardon on Calvary's tree.
I love Thee for wearing the thorns on Thy brow;
If ever I loved Thee, my Jesus, 'tis now

I'll love Thee in life, I will love Thee in death,
And praise Thee as long as Thou lendest me breath;
And say when the death dew lies cold on my brow,
If ever I loved Thee, my Jesus, 'tis now

In mansions of glory and endless delight,
I'll ever adore Thee in heaven so bright;
I'll sing with the glittering crown on my brow;
If ever I loved Thee, my Jesus, 'tis now.

(Words by William R. Featherston; music by Adoniram J. Gordon)

2. Love Others Louder. Many years ago a shabbily dressed boy trudged several miles through the snowy streets of Chicago, determined to attend a Bible class conducted by D.L. Moody. When he arrived, he was asked, "Why did you come to a Sunday school so far away? Why didn't you go to one of the churches near your home?" He answered simply, "Because you love a fellow over here."

It's not enough for us to receive the love of God and to respond with love back to Him. We are also called to love one another. The second greatest commandment is this: "Love your neighbor as yourself" (Matthew 22:39).

Who are your neighbors? Here's a simple test. First, ask yourself if they have a pulse. Next, ask yourself if they live on earth. Finally, ask yourself if they are human. If the answer to all three questions is yes (drum roll please), they are your neighbors, and you are called to love them. Remember—this commandment is second only to the command for us to love God.

How can you love your neighbor? In his book *Mere Christianity*, C.S. Lewis wrote,

> Do not waste your time bothering whether you "love" your neighbor, act as if you did. As soon as we do this, we find one of the great secrets. When you are behaving as if you loved someone, you will presently come to love him. If you injure someone you dislike, you will find yourself disliking him more. If you do him a good turn, you will find yourself disliking him less.

The Bible gives us some key instructions about loving others. Many of them can be summed up in the following two guidelines: *accept one another* and *serve one another*.

Accept one another. We need to set our expectations and disappointments aside to accept others. Jesus said, "'A new command I give you: Love one another. As I have loved you, so you must love one another. By this all men will know that you are my disciples, if you love one another'" (John 13:34-35).

How has Jesus loved us? Unconditionally. He loves us in spite of us. We have to do the same for others, by accepting them for who they are. Even the difficult people in our lives. Even the people who might not accept us! Paul told the believers in Rome, "Accept one another, then, just as Christ accepted you, in order to bring praise to God" (Romans 15:7).

Serve one another. You can love others louder by serving them. As the apostle Paul says, "Serve one another in love" (Galatians 5:13). Jesus demonstrated this principle with perfect humility throughout the gospels. He said in John 15:12-13, "My command is this: Love each other as I have loved you. Greater love has no one than this, that he lay down his life for his friends." And Paul again says that we are to offer our bodies as living sacrifices (Romans 12:1-2). Are you doing that? Do you offer yourself continually as a living sacrifice to God?

Let's throw some skin on this, friend. What does it look like for you and me to love others right here, right now? I think it's different for each of us, but I know that it starts in our homes. It begins first in our marriages and extends from there to our children. It reaches across the street to our hard-to-love neighbors, to our parents, our siblings, our (gulp) in-laws, extended family, and friends. It reaches to our churches, and then moves from there to our communities. Ultimately, our neighbor is every living human on earth. Christ loves and died for each and every person you know. And billions that you don't know.

> This is how we know what love is: Jesus Christ laid down his life for us. And we ought to lay down our lives for our brothers. If anyone has material possessions and sees his brother in need but has no pity on him, how can the love of God be in him? Dear children, let us not love with words or tongue but with actions and in truth (1 John 3:16-18).

Love *requires* action! We love others when we put our faith into action and share our wealth with those who have nothing. We love others when we replace unkind responses with kind ones. We love others when we forgive them as we have been forgiven...not according to whether they deserve our forgiveness.

The little boy who walked several miles through the snowy Chicago streets to go to D.L. Moody's Sunday school class did it because he experienced love. Love is powerful. It is life changing. God longs to use us as His love source. Ask for God's help today so you can live love louder to others.

Who comes to your mind as you read this? What do you sense the Lord is bidding you to do in response?

What About Love?

Here are a few of my favorite Scripture verses about love:

> Now we see but a poor reflection as in a mirror; then we shall see face to face. Now I know in part; then I shall know fully, even as I am fully known. And now these three remain: faith, hope and love. But the greatest of these is love (1 Corinthians 13:12-13).

> Love must be sincere. Hate what is evil; cling to what is good. Be devoted to one another in brotherly love. Honor one another above yourselves (Romans 12:9-10).

Basic life stuff here, friend. I said basic, not easy. Are you challenged? Is the Holy Spirit nudging you toward loving, accepting, and serving someone in particular? We are called to love with the love of Christ. I can almost hear you screaming at your book, "But Gwen, you don't know so-and-so. They are impossible to love! They believe ABC and they do XYZ!" To which I kindly reply, "Impossible for you, perhaps, but not impossible for Christ in you." (Breathe!) You can do everything through Christ who gives you strength (Philippians 4:13).

Final Thoughts

As I come to the end of this chapter, I'd like to lead you on a brief Scripture walk to look at what God's Word says is true about you.

You Are Loved

- His love for you is everlasting, as in…forever! No matter

who you are, where you've been, or what you've done, He just plain loves you.

The LORD appeared to us in the past, saying:
"I have loved you with an everlasting love;
I have drawn you with loving-kindness."

(JEREMIAH 31:3)

- You are the apple of His eye! (Psalm 17:8).

- He listens to your prayers and hears your cries. God's love is responsive, not passive.

I love the LORD, for he heard my voice;
he heard my cry for mercy.
Because he turned his ear to me,
I will call on him as long as I live.

(PSALM 116:1-2).

- His love for you is endless.

Your love, O LORD, reaches to the heavens,
your faithfulness to the skies.

(PSALM 36:5)

- You are highly valued, friend. Jesus spoke of your value to a crowd of many thousands:

"Are not five sparrows sold for two pennies? Yet not one of them is forgotten by God. Indeed, the very hairs of your head are all numbered. Don't be afraid; you are worth more than many sparrows" (Luke 12:6-7).

- How much does God love you? He loves you so much that He left the glorious perfection of heaven where He was worshiped and wealthy to come to a depraved, imperfect world.

For you know the grace of our Lord Jesus Christ, that though he was rich, yet for your sakes he became poor, so that you through his poverty might become rich (2 Corinthians 8:9).

The God of the universe loves you so much that he sent His Son Jesus to die for you. He who was perfectly beautiful became broken, so that we who are broken could become perfectly beautiful. That's *true* love, my friend! It is complete and perfect.

You Are Known

- God knows everything about you...and still loves you!

> For you created my inmost being;
>   you knit me together in my mother's womb.
> I praise you because I am fearfully and wonderfully made;
>   your works are wonderful,
>   I know that full well.
> My frame was not hidden from you
>   when I was made in the secret place.
> When I was woven together in the depths of the earth,
>   your eyes saw my unformed body.
> All the days ordained for me
>   were written in your book
>   before one of them came to be.
>
> (PSALM 139:13-16)

You Are Adored

- God delights in you!

> The LORD delights in those who fear him,
>   who put their hope in his unfailing love.
>
> (PSALM 147:11)

> He brought me out into a spacious place;
>   he rescued me because he delighted in me.
>
> (PSALM 18:19)

- God treasures you!

  "The Lord your God is with you,
      he is mighty to save.
  He will take great delight in you,
      he will quiet you with his love,
      he will rejoice over you with singing."

          (ZEPHANIAH 3:17)

My dear sister, do you know and accept that you are valued and adored by God? Oh, I hope you do! As we conclude this chapter, I'd like to pray the same prayer that the apostle Paul prayed for his brothers and sisters in the church of Ephesus. Let's bow our hearts before our loving Father and confidently approach His throne together:

> I pray that out of his glorious riches he may strengthen you with power through his Spirit in your inner being, so that Christ may dwell in your hearts through faith. And I pray that you, being rooted and established in love, may have power, together with all the saints, to grasp how wide and long and high and deep is the love of Christ, and to know this love that surpasses knowledge—that you may be filled to the measure of all the fullness of God.

> Now to Him who is able to do immeasurably more than all we ask or imagine, according to his power that is at work within us, to him be glory in the church and in Christ Jesus throughout all generations, for ever and ever! Amen (Ephesians 3:16-21).

"His Love Was First"

Words and music by Gwen Smith

Angels sang as one
Before His voice lit the sun
And even then He loved me
Though life had not begun
His love preceded all my hopes and dreams
It's greater than my mind can possibly conceive

His love was first
His love will last
His love forgives
Forgets the past
Before my breath
Long after death
He loves me at my best and at my worst
His love was first

People, can't you see
You can live abundantly
There's something even greater
He longs for you to be
The answer's not that far from where you are
Just take Him at His word and trust Him at His heart

His love was first
His love will last
His love forgives
Forgets the past
Before your breath
Long after death
He loves you at your best and at your worst
His love was first

When you take the hand that's reaching to you
You'll breathe deeper and life will be new

He loves you
He knows you
He wants you
He chose you

10

Got Beauty?

Praise be to the God and Father of our Lord Jesus Christ,
the Father of compassion and the God of all comfort, who comforts us
in all our troubles, so that we can comfort those in any trouble with the
comfort we ourselves have received from God.

2 CORINTHIANS 1:3-4

I love stories. Always have. I love to be moved, inspired, taught, and challenged through real-life experiences. That's probably one of the reasons why I love the Bible so much. It's the greatest compilation of stories that ever has been or ever will be written. Filled with stories that have spoken through all generations, God's Word is as relevant today as it was the day each chapter and verse was breathed into existence by His Spirit. My friend Haven says, "God's Word is as fresh as this morning's cup of coffee," and I wholeheartedly agree. Stories are powerful tools for communication.

As a little girl, I loved the occasional Sundays when missionaries came to our church. I used to sit in the red padded pews and relish the photos of unfamiliar faces and places in their slide presentations. I hung on every word they said. I was fascinated by the accounts of hardships they endured. I loved hearing about the foreign territories God had led them to. And my faith was always boosted when they told of God's powerful provision in moments of their greatest need.

The story of your life is just as fascinating. (Yes, I said *your* life.) Whether you have a past filled with pain, shame, and hardship, or whether you are blessed to have avoided the lion's share of pitfalls known to womankind, the story of God's work in your life is valuable and needs to be shared. Each of us has a story to tell.

Now, don't tune me out here! I used to be in the "Don't Ask, Don't Tell" girls club. I may as well have been the president of our local chapter. After my abortion, I was so ashamed and disturbed by the wretchedness of my choices that the very thought of telling anyone would never have entered my mind. Seriously. If you would've asked me ten years ago to share my testimony, it would've been safely constructed in a very "good Christian girl" kind of way, with vague details of "mistakes I've made" and great detail of the grace that saved me. (Are you amen-ing me?)

But God...

Don't you love those two little words?

But God had a plan for my testimony—or my *messtimony*, as I often call it. That plan was all about His glory. It was all about revealing His unconditional love and pointing to His great mercy that are available to everyone. I'm embarrassed to confess, however, that I neither approved of nor wanted His plan, even though I loved Him dearly.

You see, I thought I needed to keep my secret. I thought if I told anyone where I'd been and what I'd done, no one would ever look at me the same. Might I be so bold as to name this reluctance? P-R-I-D-E. I cared more about protecting my reputation than about proclaiming my restoration. I had a tight grasp on my story and I didn't want to release it. Selfishly, I felt that God could use me in other ways, but *not* in that way. It took many years, many girlfriends, and a revelation of my prideful ways for God to bring me to the place of surrender.

Surrender to the Call

So how did I get to the place where I was willing to write this book and speak to hundreds upon hundreds of women about the healing and forgiveness I experienced following my abortion? Kicking and screaming, that's how. But God is kind. He eased me into it. He gave me several one-on-one opportunities.

One day, about a year after my abortion, I got a call from a girl-friend who was facing an unplanned pregnancy. She was one of only a handful of friends who knew what I'd done. She was a young, sweet Christian girl who felt trapped and wanted to be set free from her "problem." Oh, how I knew that feeling! She was to start college soon and didn't want to begin classes as a pregnant unwed teen. She also didn't want to put her well-thought-of Christian parents through the embarrassment and scandal of her sinful situation.

I'll never forget the desperation in her voice on the other end of the phone. She was so scared. I wanted to hold her as she wept, but since I couldn't, I just wept with her. She called me because she needed help. She wanted me to help pay for an abortion. She and her boy-friend could come up with only a small portion of the money, and she thought, because of what I'd gone through, I would understand her predicament. I can assure you, *because of what I'd gone through,* I did understand her predicament...and that's why I had the courage to tell her no.

I told her that having an abortion was the worst mistake of my life, and that I live each day with regret because of it. I told her that I loved her and would stand by her through it all. That an abortion was not a solution to her unplanned pregnancy. That she had a chance to do what was right. I told her that she needed to have the baby.

In that moment, God gave me my first opportunity to defend an unborn life. It was terribly painful. One of the hardest conversations I've ever had. I felt like the world's biggest hypocrite. I was telling my sweet girlfriend, whom I love dearly, to endure the public shame that I didn't have the courage to face myself. I was telling her to choose life for her baby, when I had chosen death for mine.

Even as our phone conversation unfolded, I remember the enemy trying to get into my head: "What right do you have to tell her to have that baby? You're a big phony! She should be able to do what she wants to do. What kind of friend are you?" His lies came at me like shots from a semiautomatic weapon. I realized that this was war, and I was on the front lines.

She chose to have the baby and gave her up for adoption. That baby is now a wonderful teenager being raised in a loving Christian home by parents who were unable to have children of their own. Thank you, Jesus! I'm overwhelmed by gratefulness as I write this. I thank God that in that crisis moment, because of what I'd been through, I was able to relate to and minister to my dear friend. I thank God that in that crisis moment He used my story as a weapon for truth and life.

What was once a wound has become a weapon.

That was the first time God used my story to make a difference in the life of another. The second time is just as memorable. I had just turned twenty-six years old, and Brad and I had been married for three and a half years. We still lived in our college town, but our college friends had scattered across the states. Suzanne was one such friend.

She had moved away the summer that Brad and I got married, but Suzanne traveled back across the country to show up for our wedding. That's the kind of friend she is. Loyal and dependable. Even though she's only four months younger than I am, she's like a kid sister to me. We have always had a special friendship. From the start, God allowed me to encourage her in faith and in life. To be a mentor-friend.

So the night Suzanne called from Tennessee with an eerily familiar tone in her voice, I cringed.

Not again, God! I thought. *I really don't want to go there.*

"You must," He whispered to my soul.

But God, Suzanne doesn't know! She sees me as Gwen, her godly friend, not as her Gwen-who-had-an-abortion-and-keeps-it-a-secret friend!

My lamentations faded quickly as I listened to my girlfriend speak of her decision to have an abortion. Once again, I had to swallow my pride in order to speak of my painful abortion. This was life or death. What choice did I have? So I told her my story. What was a moment of surrender for me was a moment of salvation for her. Here's how she tells it:

> I struggled for days before I got up enough courage to tell the father

of the baby that I was pregnant. I will never forget the look in his eyes the moment I told him. The same feelings I had felt for days, I could now see in him. He softly whispered, "What are you going to do?" I knew at that moment by the disappointment on his face that what I thought was love was nothing more than sex and lies. I knew that I was about to go through a battle with my boyfriend, God, and myself.

A couple days passed and we met again. What he asked me to do had already been weighing on my mind and heart for days. He asked me to abort the pregnancy. He said, "I will be here for you. We will go through this together."

All I wanted was to be loved. I wondered if he would love me more if I did what he asked. I wondered if he would continue to date me. My family would never have to find out. It could be our secret, and life could be the same.

The next day I argued with God, "I did this to myself, but Lord, You let it happen! You allowed me to get pregnant! Why would you allow me to get pregnant knowing that I would be doing this alone? Why would you let this happen?"

The only thing that seemed to make sense was to abort the pregnancy. I was so disgusted with myself. I hated every minute of trying to make a decision that, no matter what I did, would change me forever. If I kept the baby, then I'd have to face the embarrassment of being single and pregnant. If I aborted the pregnancy, I'd have to face the guilt for the rest of my life.

My mind was convinced that I should have an abortion, but my heart was telling me to keep the baby. A small voice inside my soul was telling me, "Call Gwen." I said, "No! She will never understand. She'll be disappointed in me." Again, I heard a voice deep inside say, "Call Gwen. She is your sister in Christ. She loves you and she will listen."

I hesitantly picked up the phone and dialed her number. I was terrified of what she might say to me. I never expected that I would actually feel better after hanging up with her...that I would actually consider keeping the baby.

Gwen's story saved my son's life. God worked through Gwen to convince me that if I chose to abort the pregnancy, I would never be the same. I would hate myself for taking the easy way out. So I kept my baby. I prayed and asked God to watch over him and to put His shield of protection around him. God's Word says He will be a "Father to the fatherless," so I asked Him to be a Father to my son.

God watched after my son and is still watching after him. It has been eleven years since I gave birth, and I couldn't be more proud to be his mother. The road has not been easy. I still struggle with the fact that I disappointed God, but God has been faithful—even when I wasn't.

Suzanne is still a dear friend of ours. She is now married to a godly man who loves and adopted her son, and they have three other children. I'm so thankful that, for a second time, God allowed my former wound to be used as a weapon for truth.

Accept the Call

I'll never forget the first time I heard a woman in ministry talk about the abortion she had. I was at a women's conference for Proverbs 31 Ministries (www.proverbs31.org), serving as their worship leader. After I finished leading worship, I walked off stage and grabbed a seat near the back of the room. Lysa TerKeurst, the ministry's president, took the stage and began to speak. Her warmth as a speaker immediately drew us in. She's funny, expressive, adorable, and articulate. I mean, the girl can flat-out tell a story! So as she transitioned to her testimony, every eye in the house was focused on Lysa. We were all moved as she told us of some painful trials she had endured as a child and of a rebellious season she went through in her late teens. Then, *whack!* She told hundreds of women that she had had an abortion.

I was so stunned to hear her confession that I don't remember hearing anything else she said. My mind reeled. *She had an abortion. Another woman in ministry actually had an abortion. I'm not the only one! But, oh my mercy, she just said it out loud! Does she* know *that she just said that out loud? In front of all these women?*

I was so overwhelmed by her courage and inspired by her story of healing that my soul began to jump up and down exclaiming, *Me too! I've been there! I've been forgiven and set free too! Amen, sister!*

Hallelujah! God is so good! At the very same time, my mind told my soul, *Sit down and be quiet!*

As I sat there, I witnessed the power of God at work through Lysa. I realized that He was using her story to pour out healing to the women who listened. I sensed the presence and movement of the Spirit of God as women all around the room allowed chains of shame to fall from their hearts. It was almost a visible emancipation.

That night, God took a shovel to the soil of stubbornness in my heart and began a groundbreaking first dig. "Come on Gwen," He seemed to say. "See what's going on here? I've got a plan and you are a part of it. Trust me! Loosen your grip on that story of yours because I'm going to need it to complete My plan."

A wrestling match began that night between God and me. Sadly, it went on for many months. Have I mentioned that I'm a bit stubborn? I was scared. I felt like the cowardly lion in *The Wizard of Oz*. I tried to reason with God, *You already have wonderful Christian women like Lysa to tell her story. You don't need me for that. I'm a worshiper! I write songs! We're good here, right?*

I tried to run away from my assignment just as the Old Testament prophet Jonah tried to run from his. The call from God for me to publicly share my abortion story was Jonah's call to Nineveh—the very place I didn't want to go.

Lucky for me, I didn't get swallowed up by a big fish. I did, however, get swallowed up by conviction from the Holy Spirit. God did not back down when I resisted His leading, even though for a while I tried to ignore His call. The wrestling match continued…and God was winning.

It took a year and a half for me to surrender. A key conversation led me to my turning point. And, as God would have it, what He started with Lysa's testimony, He sealed with Lysa's testimony.

In the fall of 2005, Lysa and I were booked to minister together at a women's retreat. The opening session was exciting. God's presence was very evident in the worship, and the women were ripe and ready to hear from Him through Lysa's message. When Lysa took the stage and told her story, once again I witnessed God's power and God's passion. God gives us His power to minister through our brokenness because He is passionate about restoring wounded hearts. As I listened for the second time to Lysa tell of her abortion, I *knew* deep down that God was calling me to do the same thing.

After the session, Lysa and I went to her room to hang out. We were both excited about what God had done that night and were eager to see what else He had in store that weekend. Our conversation eventually led to her testimony, so I asked her, "Do you think that just because we're in public ministry that we're obligated to tell people everything we've ever done?"

"Not at all," she said.

Excellent! I thought. *I'm off the hook!*

"We don't have to tell people everything we've been through," she continued, "*but* we need to be willing if God calls us to. Then, yes—we *are* obligated to tell."

With that, God pinned me to the mat. And as much as the lion-with-no-courage in me wanted to think otherwise back then, I now concur wholeheartedly with Lysa's wisdom. It's God's wisdom. It's God's plan. We don't have to tell our stories to anybody...*unless* God leads us to. Then we must be willing. God has given us the task of reconciling people to Him. The Bible says it this way:

> This means that anyone who belongs to Christ has become a new person. The old life is gone; a new life has begun!
>
> And all of this is a gift from God, who brought us back to himself through Christ. And God has given us this task of reconciling people to him. For God was in Christ, reconciling the world to himself, no longer counting people's sins against them. And he gave us this wonderful message of reconciliation. *So we are Christ's ambassadors; God is making his appeal through us.* We speak for Christ when we plead, "Come back to God!" (2 Corinthians 5:17-20, NLT, emphasis added).

After all that Jesus has done for us, each of us has the opportunity to do something for Him. You are Christ's ambassador. Yes, it requires courage. Yes, it means you must lay down your pride. But trust this: beauty and blessing follow the surrender, and God is faithful to equip the messenger. God wants you to move beyond your comfort to your call.

I love this prayer attributed to the sixteenth-century explorer and naval pioneer Sir Francis Drake:

> Disturb us, Lord, when we are too well pleased with ourselves, when our dreams have come true because we have dreamed too little, when we arrive safely because we have sailed too close to the shore. Disturb us, Lord, when with the abundance of things we possess, we have lost our thirst for the waters of life; having fallen in love with life, we have ceased to dream of eternity; and in our efforts to build a new Earth, we have allowed our vision of the new heaven to dim. Disturb us, Lord, to dare more boldly, to venture on wider seas where storms will show your mastery; where losing sight of land, we shall find the stars. We ask you to push back the horizons of our hopes; and to push into the future in strength, courage, hope, and love.

A Willing Heart

My husband, Brad, went on a mission trip to Guatemala last year. What he saw and experienced changed his life and increased his faith in a dramatic way. He was an eyewitness to the healing power of God. On that trip he prayed harder, believed more, and expected more from God each passing day—and as a result, God used their medical missions team as a conduit for miracles.

You and I have that same opportunity every day. We have a chance to be a witness of God's healing love to a world of wounded hearts. Did God need my husband and the other volunteers to heal Guatemalan villagers, treat their physical wounds, and share the hope of Jesus with them? No. Did God move in the lives of the villagers because of the team's willingness to go in His name? You bet!

Hector, the founder of that Guatemalan ministry, recently visited North Carolina, and my family and I went to hear him speak. When I heard him testify of the provision and power of God, my heart was stirred and my faith was boosted. But what moved me most was the story of the lesson he learned about his call after God led him to be a medical missionary.

Before he began the medical ministry that he devotes his life to now, Hector's main goal in life was to make lots of money. Back then he didn't even apologize for it. He was a Christian and figured that God could use his money to help others.

Back in the late eighties, Hector and his wife joined a medical team on a mission to a mountain village. The team was blown away by what God did through them while they were there, so on the four-hour drive back to the city, they worshiped and sang praises to God.

As he worshiped and drove, Hector heard the Lord speak to his soul. "This is what I've made you for. To medically treat My people, to pray for their healing, and to share the hope of Jesus with the hopeless and the lost."

Hector felt so overwhelmed that he pulled the truck over and told the team of his call from God to be a missionary doctor. They prayed over him, whooped it up in celebration, and then continued down the mountain with an even greater sense of purpose and excitement. Hector thought that God had called him to be a missionary because of his skills as a doctor. Later, he would think otherwise.

A few years into his work, while visiting a remote village, a woman with a large mass on her side came into their makeshift clinic. Her terrible pain was curbed only by her excitement that the medical team had come to help her. One glance at her tumor and Hector had a strong suspicion that it was malignant. Upon examining her further, Hector was convinced that she was terminal. He became frustrated with God because he couldn't do anything to help her physically, to the extent that he didn't even want to share the gospel with her.

Hector sent up a few prayers of frustration, but felt God nudging him to share the gospel with this woman. So he reluctantly shared the good news of Jesus with her, and, to Hector's surprise, she wanted to pray to receive Christ! And as they sat on the floor of that makeshift med-center, this sweet woman trusted Jesus as her Savior.

When they finished praying, the woman had a radiant smile and tears in her eyes. He hugged her and she began to cry.

"What happened?" Hector asked. "Why are you crying?"

"As we were praying," she said, "I felt a warmth that started on my head and spread to the tips of my toes." As she said this, she realized something had changed, and she screamed with delight. "My mass is gone! My pain is gone!"

Hector had her lie back down on his examining table. The tumor that had been there just minutes ago was gone. God had intervened. She was healed, both spiritually and physically!

In the amazing celebration that followed, God spoke clearly to Hector's heart. God told him that He had all the power needed for the work He had called Hector to, and it had nothing to do with his medical training. God didn't need Hector's skills or his knowledge, He had all of that covered. He just wanted him to go in His name.

One of my favorite sayings is, "God doesn't call the equipped, He equips the called." If you are His, then you are called. Not because of who you are or what you can do, but because God can and will do His work through you.

Did God tell Jonah to go to Nineveh because Jonah was a great leader with amazing vision? No! Jonah proved to be quite wimpy. When Jonah finally made it to Nineveh, did God bring a great wave of repentance and restoration because of Jonah's rhetorical gifts? No! God stirred the hearts and changed the lives of hundreds of Ninevites because Jonah finally had the courage to speak God's words.

God wants to do something similar through you.

He wants you to stop fighting Him on this and be willing to speak for Him so others can know the same healing that you know. He wants to bring beauty up from the ashes of brokenness all around you.

Not Now, God!

After the final session at a recent three-day ministry event, I was focused and fervent, determined to head home to my husband and three children as quickly as possible. I busied myself wrapping microphone chords, loading CDs from my resource table, and prepping to leave. While I was mid-busy, a friendly thirty-something woman I'd chatted with previously that weekend came up to me with her friend. I was courteous to them, but in a "see-you-later" kind of way.

Not getting my subtle clues, this woman inquired excitedly about the book I was writing. (Yes, that would be this book.) I lifted my head with surprise as she announced, "I can't wait to read your book! Your enthusiasm for the Lord is so contagious, and I just know you have an amazing testimony!" Then she and her friend stood there expectantly.

Okay, feel my pain here. It is *day three* of a three-day event! I am exhausted. I am done. Yet this woman and her friend want to hear my testimony. So, I did what any normal fleshy woman would do. I told God, *Not now, Lord. I'm going home. I've done what I came to do and now I'm going home to my family. I'm tired, slightly grumpy, definitely hungry, and done. I can't tell these girls about my abortion right now. Nope. Not going to go there. Please don't ask me to!*

So I looked up at these two sweet women and, with a forced chuckle, said, "Yeah, I've got a doozy of a story, but don't we all? Thank God for grace."

There! Now they should leave me alone, I thought.

But God kept nudging my heart. "Tell them, Gwen."

Before I had a chance to continue my dialog with the Lord, another couple of women came to join our conversation. I was so not amused.

God, are You kidding me? We are done here!

But He kept nudging.

So I finally conceded and shared my testimony with the six women who had gathered to speak to me. Within minutes, two of the six were crying. They'd had abortions as well and for years had lived under the weight of shame. We became a bonded band of blubbering sisters. The story of my redemption from brokenness, the beauty and healing I found in Christ, became a tool in the hands of God that afternoon. Once again, what had been a wound became a weapon.

Melissa was one of my sweet sisters who found forgiveness during that conversation. Here's her account of what happened:

My husband and I have been married almost seven years now and have been unsuccessful in getting pregnant. As the years pass, I've found myself wondering if we've not been blessed with a child because of my abortion. Part of my heart accepted this lot as my punishment for my horrible decision, while the other thought it just didn't sound like the God I'd grown to love and worship. Coupled with these feelings, I'd known God had some type of special ministry for me, though He had not yet revealed it. And then I met Gwen.

The women's conference had just ended, and I was in the middle of a conversation with someone. The Lord led me from that conversation to one that Gwen was having with a few other women. She was telling her testimony. I cried as I heard her story. Here before me stood a woman, in the ministry no less, who shared my shame. I just couldn't believe it, and I knew at that moment why God had led me to attend that conference. God opened my eyes to see that He can and will use any willing vessel, no matter what shame might exist in the past. Before me stood living proof of God's contagious love, joy, and mercy.

I told Gwen that we shared the same past and that I have been unable to have children. She and the others present immediately gathered around me with prayers of love and support. That day, I forgave myself for aborting my baby. I knew God had forgiven me, but I had not yet taken the step to forgive myself. I realize now that God has not been punishing me by making me barren; it simply has not been His time.

God changed my life that day because He gave a woman the courage to share her story. It made me realize that I, too, have a story to tell. To share with other women who feel helpless, lost, at the end of their rope. The message of God's love, grace, mercy, fulfillment, and healing is what the Christian walk is all about.

Brokenness. We don't want it, but we've all got it. When our brokenness is surrendered to God, restoration begins and beauty blossoms. He restores our wounded hearts with His unconditional love. This exciting, life-changing truth should make even the most conservative Christ-follower want to jump up and shout, "Hallelujah!"

Do you get it? What we do with our restored hearts makes all the difference.

Got beauty? What are you going to do with it?

Your Story Can Help Others

Have you been forgiven much? Have you experienced His healing? It's time for us to stop pretending, to step out from behind the cardboard paper dolls we like to hide behind. Even to this day I get a bit nervous each time I take the stage to share my story. I have to swat away insecurities that fly in my face by reminding myself that God wants to reveal His love to others through me. And He wants to do the same through you...through your story...through the beauty that you reflect as a woman who has been transformed by unconditional love. Look at these Scripture verses that challenge us this way:

> Has the LORD redeemed you? *Then speak out!*
> *Tell others* he has redeemed you from your enemies.
>
> (PSALM 107:2, NLT, EMPHASIS ADDED)

> But in your hearts set apart Christ as Lord. *Always be prepared to give an answer to everyone who asks you to give the reason for the hope that you have.* But do this with gentleness and respect, keeping a clear conscience, so that those who speak maliciously against your good behavior in Christ may be ashamed of their slander (1 Peter 3:15-16, emphasis added).

> *I proclaim* righteousness in the great assembly;
> 　*I do not seal my lips,*
> 　as you know, O LORD.
> *I do not hide* your righteousness in my heart;
> 　*I speak* of your faithfulness and salvation.

I do not conceal your love and your truth
from the great assembly.

(PSALM 40:9-10, EMPHASIS ADDED)

The heartfelt *counsel of a friend*
is as sweet as perfume and incense.

(PROVERBS 27:9, NLT, EMPHASIS ADDED)

Two are better than one,
because they have a good return for their work:
If one falls down,
his friend can help him up.
But pity the man who falls
and has no one to help him up!

(ECCLESIASTES 4:10, EMPHASIS ADDED)

The Spirit of the Sovereign LORD is on me,
because the LORD has anointed me
to preach good news to the poor.
He has sent me to bind up the brokenhearted,
to proclaim freedom for the captives
and release from darkness for the prisoners.

(ISAIAH 61:1, EMPHASIS ADDED)

God calls each of us to use our lives to point to His hope. Right before He ascended into heaven, Jesus said, "But you will receive power when the Holy Spirit comes on you; and *you will be my witnesses* in Jerusalem, and in all Judea and Samaria, and to the ends of the earth" (Acts 1:8, emphasis added). That call—that commission—will look different for each of us. While some might be called to share before groups of women or large congregations, many of us are called to share with a friend who is hurting, with a woman who is struggling to know freedom, with a sister who needs to hear that healing and forgiveness are always possible with God.

Whether you've had an abortion or lost a baby through a miscarriage—whether you've been sexually abused or have had an affair—whether you are divorced, widowed, single, or married—whether you've experienced infertility, infidelity, or insecurity—God can use your story to help others. If you have a child or spouse with a disability, if you battle depression, illness, a drug or alcohol addiction, have an eating disorder or anger management problems, God can use your story.

However God leads you, I pray that you will not hesitate to tell others about the brokenness you have encountered and the beauty you now know in Christ. Use your life as a living testimony of God's transforming power, "being confident of this, that He who began a good work in you will carry it on to completion until the day of Christ Jesus" (Philippians 1:6). Ultimately, the love of God that radiates from your story will result in a reflection of that love back to God and to others who are in desperate need of His healing.

My prayer is that every day you will become less broken and more beautiful as you experience the God who transforms us from "worthless into precious, guilty to forgiven, hungry into satisfied, and empty into full." In every broken circumstance you face, I encourage you to remember grace, believe truth, run to Jesus, seek His heart, and find restoration in His unconditional love.

He's the only One who can change your broken into beautiful.

Thrive in His beauty, my friend.

"Justified"

Words by Gwen Smith
Music by Gwen Smith and Robert Cowherd

I'm justified
I've been set free
The law of sin has no hold on me
I'm sanctified
In Jesus' name
Declared not guilty
There is no blame

Alive in Christ, a new creation
I'll share His love with no hesitation
I'm justified, I've been set free
In Christ I find my identity
I'm justified in Christ

Notes

1. Robert S. McGee, *The Search for Significance* (Nashville: W Publishing Group, 1998), 6.

2. John Piper, "When Satan Hurts Christ's People," © 2007 Desiring God, www.DesiringGod.org.

3. *Life Application Bible,* New International Version (Wheaton, Ill.: Tyndale House Publishers and Grand Rapids, Mich.: Zondervan), 423.

4. Featured on the *Because* CD by Gwen Smith (www.GwenSmith.net) © Sunday Best Music/ (ASCAP) Newspring, a division of Zomba Enterprises, Inc. (ASCAP)/ CCTB Music (ASCAP). All rights OBO CCTB. Music administered by New Spring. Used by permission.

5. Joseph Stowell, *Fan the Flame* (Chicago: Moody Press, 1986), 119.

6. Tim Hansel, *Eating Problems for Breakfast* (Waco, Tex.: Word Publishing, 1988), 39.

To learn more about books by Harvest House Publishers
or to read sample chapters, log on to our website:
www.harvesthousepublishers.com

HARVEST HOUSE PUBLISHERS
EUGENE, OREGON

About the Author

Gwen Smith and her husband, Brad, live in Charlotte, North Carolina where they are raising three tall teens (who keep them on their toes and on their knees). She speaks and leads worship at events around the country and is the author of several books. Gwen is also the cofounder of Girlfriends in God, a relatable, Jesus-centered conference and devotional ministry that encourages and equips women in their spiritual journey.

Check out her ministry, schedule, and blog at
www.GwenSmith.net

Connect with her on Twitter at
@GwenSmithMusic or on
Facebook.com/GwenSmithMusic